DOWN THE DECADES

with the BRITISH SOUTH AFRICA POLICE

Alan Stock & John Berry

TSL Publications

BOOKS OF THE BRITISH SOUTH AFRICA POLICE

The Great War in Africa Association

Reprinted and published in Great Britain in 2022

By Great War in Africa Association, TSL Publications, Rickmansworth

ISBN: 978-1-914245-69-5

First published in 2007 and 2011 by the United Kingdom Branch of the British South Africa Police Regimental Association.

Acknowledgement and thanks go to:
National Archives of Zimbabwe
The Outpost Magazine of the British South Africa Police
Cover Design: Alan Toms (7391)
Books of the B.S.A.P. Crest Design: Les Burrows (9591)
The History Section Committee, United Kingdom Branch of the
Regimental Association. Chairman Alan Toms
Alan Stock (6063), was Editor of *The Outpost* from 1966 to 1984
Originally arranged and typeset by John Berry (5584)

Apology is made for standard of some photographs. This is caused by scanning from old magazines with poor paper quality.

In reprinting this text, no changes have been made to the language used as it historically reflects the time. It is recognised that some terminology is deemed inappropriate today and it is hoped that readers will accept the text for the historical document it is and that offense is not intended.

CONTENTS

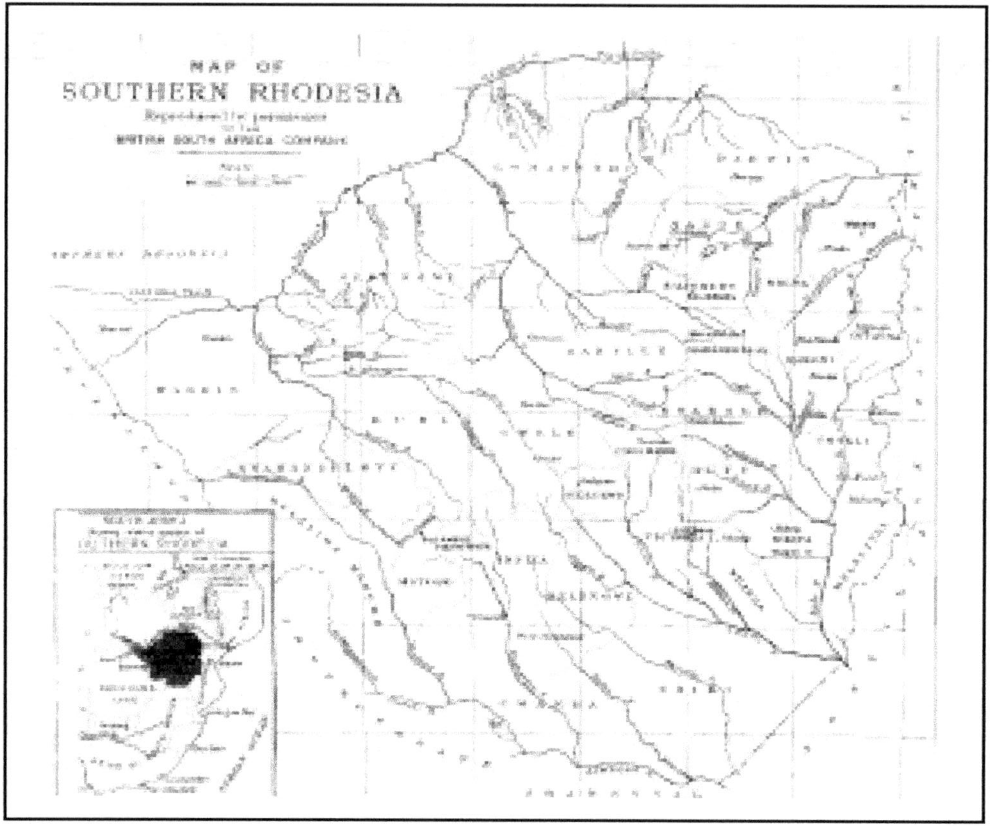
MAP OF
SOUTHERN RHODESIA

INTRODUCTION

From 1890, the British South Africa Company's Police, later to become the British South Africa Police, was tasked with the policing of the territories between the Limpopo and Zambesi Rivers and between Portuguese East Africa (later Mozambique) and the territory which later became Bechuanaland then Botswana. The B.S.A.C.P. had originally been formed in 1889 to escort the Pioneer Column into Mashonaland. (See *The History of the British South Africa Police*, by Gibbs and Phillips).

These territories became known in succession as Southern Rhodesia, Rhodesia, Zimbabwe-Rhodesia and, finally, Zimbabwe, as the political situation changed.

In 1980, the B.S.A.P. became known as the Zimbabwe Republic Police and an era came to an end.

The articles in this book were selected to show the evolution of the B.S.A.P. from a Mounted Infantry Regiment to a modern Police Force, and are very, very far from being comprehensive.

Alan Stock, long-time editor of *The Outpost*, provided some of the material, while the rest was taken from *The Outpost* and some unpublished memoirs.

John Berry, 5584
May, 2007.

In compiling this second edition, the opportunity was taken to make extensive revisions, removing some articles which were later republished in other books in the Series. Some new accounts were added and also many additional photographs.

John Berry 2010

1890s

PIONEER EXPEDITION, Mashonaland, 1890

C.H. Divine,
Corporal No. 378 British South Africa Company Police

Only once did I come into actual contact with the great Cecil Rhodes and his *Fidus Achates*, Dr Jameson. I was a member of a deputation of troopers who interviewed these gentlemen at Salisbury with regard to our promised mining rights.

This was a most informal meeting. Native huts had been built for the accommodation of Rhodes and Jameson who were only in Salisbury, at that time merely an armed camp, for a short while. The deputation gathered outside Rhodes' hut at 8 a.m. one morning; he came out, fastening his braces, as he was just dressing, and listened to what our spokesman had to say, then called out, 'Jameson, come and listen to what these chaps have to say.' Out came the doctor with his face all lathered and a razor in his hand. After our man had finished the two chiefs consulted, without leaving us, and after a few questions, granted all we had asked for and we went away quite satisfied, leaving them to finish their toilets.

I have at various times contributed to the Rhodesian papers personal reminiscences of our trek north from Tuli. This trek was made under the most appalling conditions in the middle of a very bad rainy season with flooded rivers to cross and shortages of food and clothing. Of necessity in relating personal experiences the ego must be prominent, but you will make allowances for this.

Our native servants and wagon drivers were recruited from Khama's people, who lived in deadly fear of the Matabele, who were the dominant native race under the great Lobengula, and we were very short of help as natives were scared to go north. At one time I drove a team of sixteen oxen yoked to a heavy transport wagon owing to the shortage of friendly natives. Our first experience of lions on the trek came after we had halted one night. The wagons were parked in a clearing in the bush; the horses picketed to a rope stretched between two trees. Each mess of from eight to ten men had their fire round which they sat and had their evening meal. Soon the camp was still, everybody except the guard asleep, and fires dying down. About midnight from close at hand the tremendous roar of a lion was re-echoed by other lions. The effect was electrical, crouching figures of men from the outside edges of the bivouac could be seen creeping in towards the wagons. Fresh wood was piled on the fires, and soon the scene was brilliantly lit up. The armed guard over the horses climbed up a tree; all our rifles were kept handy and no one slept. The lions prowled around for a couple of hours, keeping up a racket, but evidently the bright fires kept them off and eventually all was quiet again and we were able to sleep. On another occasion the troop was riding along at ease when suddenly a huge lion jumped into the road and faced them at a distance of about thirty yards. Every horse stopped instantly, the surprise was mutual; for a couple of seconds no one moved, then Leo gave a growl and dashed into the bush. The tension relaxed, every man unslung his rifle and, headed by our Captain, spurred off after him, but he was not seen again.

On still another occasion a lioness got one of our donkeys, killed and left it. Knowing that it would return to its kill, three of our men lay under a wagon close by and waited. Sure enough she came back and was just starting on the donkey when all three fired together and got her. I watched the skinning operation and was amazed to see the enormous neck and forearm muscles. No wonder a lion can drag a full grown ox.

We had rain and almost impassable roads and rivers, but plodded on until we came to the Lundi River. We arrived at about 11 a.m. on a fine day and there was only about three feet of water in the drift. It is an axiom in South Africa to cross a river before outspanning in the rainy season, because rain many miles away will cause a river to 'come down' as we say in this country. This day, however, we had had a long hard trek and men and animals were tired, so our O/C. decided to stop on the aouth side of the stream for the mid-day halt. About 3 p.m. just as we were about to pack up, the river rose and we found there was a rushing wall of water seven feet deep at the ford. This made it impossible for us to cross with our transport. As we were running short of food, it was decided that all men with horses were to be got across somehow and to proceed with all speed to Fort Victoria, which was about 30 to 40 miles away.

Now came the job of crossing. I had been champion swimmer

of Table Bay and was pretty useful in the water, so was called upon to take the first horse across on a long lead. I went up the bank some distance and took off while the horse was 'persuaded' by my comrades to follow me. I was lucky to strike the ford on the other side, and handing over the animal to a trooper in charge of a dispatch riding post on the north bank, returned to help men, horses, arms and ammunition over. By the time it got dark I had made about half a dozen crossings, the last nearly finishing me. I was loaded with a rifle strapped to my back, and two bandoliers of ammunition, and was assisting a poor swimmer. This was too much for me and I was failing fast when my feet touched bottom. I had to rest for some time before I risked the return. Of course other good swimmers were doing the same as I was, and some non-swimmers very pluckily swam their horses across safely. It was dark when the mounted men all got over and after having dried their clothes and themselves with the aid of a huge fire, gave three cheers and pushed off into the dark.

Now arose the problem of getting the rest of the Force over the river. As I have said before, we were short of food and there was no possibility of getting help crossing from either north or aouth as the rivers were impassable. Fortunately we had a very long strong coil of rope with us, and Sergeant C. Judge and I were asked to get this across. We made a light line of tent ropes and ox reims, and making a loop to go over our shoulders, we plunged in and after a struggle got over to the other side, then hauled over the heavy rope, which had been fastened to the light line, and secured it to a tree. Someone now had a brainwave, and we proceeded to construct a raft. We had three good-sized barrels with us. These had contained the rum and lime juice rations. With tent poles lashed across these, we had a three-cornered raft. For a floor we put more tent poles across and in the centre a very large packing case which had contained saddlery. There was our raft completed. She floated beautifully. We fastened a loop from the raft to the big rope and so had a safe means of communication with the opposite shore. The passage of the first load over, which consisted mainly of tents, was anxiously watched, but all went well, so from early morn to dewy eve our ferry worked at high pressure. Only once did it capsize, that, fortunately, close to shore, and the cargo was all recovered by diving.

Now came the biggest problem of all – how to get the oxen and wagons over. We decided to experiment. Thirty-six oxen were

Crossing the Lundi River

in-spanned to a wagon, a strong rope being tied to the trek chain between the leading oxen. Fifty men were sent over by the ferry and tailed on to the end of this rope to keep the team straight on their passage. Thirty oxen were already swimming, the last six still on their feet, when the strain proved too great for the rope, which parted, and away went the oxen down the stream to certain death as we thought. We at once cut the trek chain in front of the last six oxen, meaning to save these at least. Fortunately there was an island in the middle of the river below the drift, though submerged. Some trees on it caught the middle of the team and held. The two ends came round and there was a milling mass of thirty oxen slowly drowning. We looked at each other in consternation, then one of my companions, Peter Forest Hall, came up to me with an open knife in his hand, saying: 'Charlie, you can't see those poor animals drown, won't you try to cut them loose?' I looked at my commanding officer, Captain Chamley-Turner, one of the finest men who ever lived, and he looked at me, but gave me no order as things looked too dangerous. Peter, however, persisted, so I went up the river some way, got in, and allowed the current to drift me down. I got on to the nearest ox's back and cut him loose, and as he drifted away I clambered on to another back and did the same. When I had managed to free a few this way, two other men joined me and we soon had all the oxen free. By great good fortune a little further down, the river took a sharp turn and there was a nice backwater. The half-drowned cattle struck this and all got safely ashore on the same side on which they had started; very little the worse for their terrifying experience. Finally we got all the transport oxen across by taking them well up the stream and driving them into the river, while a number of us, swimming on the lower edge, by shouting and splashing, kept them from breaking back. In this way all of them got safely over. The wagons were pulled over empty by a crowd of men with a long rope, they having crossed to the north bank by the ferry.

I saw one evening what was to me an amazing sight. It was Christmas Eve and most of the personnel were by this time camped on the north bank, some of the wagons being still on the south side. One was carrying the remains of the rum ration, so reduced that no issue had been made for some time. Suddenly the totally unexpected bugle call of 'Rum ration' rang out. The excitement was great and immediately a rush was made for the ferry, each man carrying his tin pannikin. The ferry could of course only take about five men at a time, so the crowd, non-swimmers for the most, crossed by going hand over hand along the connecting rope. As I did not take liquor it was strange to see what men would do for a drink, as it must be understood that the Lundi River was in flood and crocodiles and hippopotami were known to be in it, yet the men took a chance like this. However, I suppose the unaccustomed noise and bustle on the banks kept both crocodiles and hippos away and all was well.

After a few days on the north bank to get the transport in order, we packed up and resumed our trek. Our Captain took some of the swimmers ahead for us to see what the next river, the Tokwe, was like. We found this river running in two channels, one fairly shallow, and the other fairly deep. The Skipper thought we ought to get a rope across the deep channel, which was fortunately not very wide. The Tokwe had a bad reputation for crocodiles and when I went in, the only white man with four natives, who were from the Cape Colony and who could swim, I was really scared as it was dark when we went in. I said to the natives, 'Are you not frightened of crocodiles?' They answered quite cheerfully, 'No baas, as long as there is a white man with us it is alright, a crocodile will always take a white man first.' This was not very cheering to me; however, we got through without any trouble. A couple of days before we got to this river a man named DeRooke was standing on a rock in the same drift that we were in, encouraging his team of oxen drawing his wagon across, when a crocodile seized him by the ankle and dragged him into the river. He struggled and managed to get away on to an island. This happened at midnight and his comrades could not go to his assistance, so he had to lie there until morning. We had no doctor and at Fort Victoria, 20 miles away, there was only a trooper who had been a doctor but had lost his diploma through malpractice. This man came down and dressed DeRooke's mangled ankle, but said the unfortunate sufferer must be brought in to Fort Victoria. On arrival at the Fort gangrene had set in and there only remained amputation. There were no anaesthetics and no instruments, so the position was put to DeRooke, who said, 'Go on with it, but give me something to smoke.' So septic had the leg become that the amputation had to be done at the top of the thigh. A tenon saw and an ordinary razor were the instruments used and I was told that the operation was very cleverly done, but it was too late unfortunately and the poor fellow died.

Another incident; one of our natives was washing clothes when a crocodile caught him by the thumb. Luckily this was bitten off and the boy escaped and actually went across to the other side of the river to have his hand dressed. Small wonder that I was scared.

By the time the troop reached this river, it had fallen considerably and we rushed the transport across without much trouble and so up and on and over 'Providential Pass' to Fort Victoria, where we were very thankful to arrive and to get fresh supplies of food.

This ended the first stage of our long trek. We still had a long way to go, as our destination was Fort Charter, about 60 miles aouth of Fort Salisbury.

After recuperating for a few days at Fort Victoria we resumed our journey northwards. We were now on a plateau (mesa), having climbed steadily from the Tokwe River to Fort Victoria, the country was easier to travel over, with the exception of two rivers just outside Victoria, no big streams to hold us up. We plodded on steadily day after day through rain and muddy roads till at last one afternoon we topped a rise and there, some miles across a valley, we saw a number of native huts on a ridge and were told that that was Fort Charter, our objective.

There now descended on us one of the worst thunderstorms it has ever been my lot to experience, and I have been in a large number. It was no good stopping – we had 80 men ill with malaria riding on the transport wagons and we had to get them to shelter as soon as possible. This was indeed a nightmare of a trek – everyone was of course wet to the skin and the roads were like running rivers. We got to the camp just at dark. Fortunately the troops who had been at Charter before us had built a number of native huts and into these everybody hurried, the sick men being made as comfortable as possible. No supper of course, except a couple of army biscuits and no medicine for the sick – what a night.

Fortunately the next day was fine and our spirits rose and we were able to dry our kits and our blankets. Sergeant C. Judge was sent off to Salisbury, 60 miles away, with an urgent demand for quinine, when he returned it was with only a small quantity, as Salisbury needed the stuff as badly as we did.

After a couple of days settling in, my Captain, Chamley-Turner, sent for me and told me he wanted me to take some men and go out into the bush to cut poles to build a hospital. I picked my party and away we went some miles from camp. We found the best trees for our purpose at the edge of a large swamp and there we pitched our little patrol tents – little low things that just held two men. We worked hard and got on with the job, but what a time we had with mosquitoes – they were dreadful. At night when we turned in we took two plates of live coals from the fire. Covering these with green leaves, we then placed one plate between us at our heads and the other at our feet and closed the tent door as tight as possible. If we could get to sleep before the smudge fire failed, all was well; if not, then it meant a sleepless night. Such mosquitoes I had never before encountered. I think they must have been about three to the pound – they certainly felt like it.

One of my men, Bob Gracie, shot a leopard from the tent door. We were very glad when we finished the job and got back to the comparatively comfortable camp at Fort Charter – it was certainly no picnic for us. Soon after getting back Captain Turner again sent for me and addressed me as follows: 'Divine, you know how things are here – very little food and no prospects of any more reaching us from either north or south for some time – I want you to take a small party and go out to the native kraals and see what you can get in the way of food-stuffs. We have got a little trading stuff such as limbo, beads and salt. See what you can get by barter. I want you to get food, fairly if possible, but (here he paused impressively) always remember that food we must have. Choose your own men and take the necessary horses.'

This was some job for me, but of course there was nothing to be said about it, I just had to do the best I could. I should explain that we had some oxen which we killed for meat, but these were all suffering from 'lung sickness' and when cooked an enormous amount of liquid came out of the meat and altogether it was very unpleasant eating. The men complained to the doctor who

Fort Charter

was with us, Dr Grogan, who, while sympathising with us, said that the meat would not harm us. The troops were too sick and the country too wet to go game hunting.

I picked three men, all of whom were only too glad to go with me and get away from the Fort and the atmosphere round it, which was anything but cheerful. We rode off, not knowing where we were going, nor how we were going to fare. We followed the one main road until we struck a kaffir path going across it. This path we followed, knowing that it would bring us to a native village.

Natives in their natural state always walk in single file, thus a path is made between points and followed slavishly, so that it becomes unbelievably hard considering that it is worn down by bare feet. Rhodesia in those days was honeycombed by these Kaffir paths and very useful we found them, though of course we also could only get along in single file.

About 20 miles from the Fort we struck our first native village, and what excitement we caused! Few of the natives had seen white men before and the horses caused tremendous curiosity and alarm. At first, with the exception of a few old men, the natives ran away and hid themselves, but we soon convinced those who remained of our peaceful intentions, so they called to the others and gradually they drifted back and we were soon surrounded, at a respectable distance, by the whole population of the kraal.

I had with me a trooper who had been a trader amongst the Kaffirs of the Cape Colony; and he told the chief the object of our visit. Before starting I stipulated that for everything we bought containers were to be lent us and men to carry the supplies to Fort Charter, promising that every man who brought his load to the Fort would be given payment in trade goods. All this was agreed to. We then started; we displayed our stock, and the crowd dispersed to collect the various commodities they had for sale. Chattering like monkeys, they were soon back carrying all sorts of things, pumpkins, pink rice, mealies on the cob and in the grain, a small kind of vegetable marrow, monkey nuts, eggs (very small and of doubtful vintage) and Kaffir corn, a small round grain which when ground made excellent porridge. The sight of all this green food was very welcome to us, vegetable starved troopers as we were.

It took a long time to conclude the first sale by barter, as the natives were not altogether trusting us, but after seeing that the first ones to sell got a fair deal, they got the selling fever and fairly rushed us, and it took the four of us all our time to cope with the business on hand. Our salt was in great demand and the women wanted the cheap calico cloth and cornelian beads and brassware.

When we got enough to load 20 carriers, I stopped the sale, much to the disgust of latecomers. Then I asked the chief for containers, consisting mostly of fibre bags and grass baskets, and men to carry them. To my annoyance I found that all the able-bodied men had drifted away and also that no bags or baskets were forthcoming. I was furious at being done down like this, but was determined that the provisions should reach Charter. I left one man in charge of the goods, and with the other two, drew revolvers and entered every little round hut and made a prisoner of every man we could find and took possession of what bags and baskets we needed. We took each man we got and handed him over to the guard. I heard a shout and rushing into a hut I found two men attacking one of my troopers. A revolver shot fired over their heads soon brought them to their senses and we had little further trouble.

We got our 20 men and not wanting any further delay, I apportioned the loads and told off two of my men to take the convoy into camp, while I and the other man remained behind, warning the natives that if a single load was thrown away on the journey I would burn their village. This threat had the desired result, every load was safely delivered, and each bearer was suitably rewarded. I was never caught like this again.

At this time every Mashona village was built on a kopje, generally very rocky and was encompassed by a very heavy stockade. There were usually two openings which were closed at night, after what little livestock – cattle and goats – they possessed, had been driven in from the grazing grounds. The reason for this was that before the advent of the Pioneer Expedition, the powerful and war-like Matabele tribe under Lobengula had been in the habit of raiding the Mashona every year, taking cattle, women and children – so for protection they had to live on hills within stockaded villages.

In our subsequent tradings I always took up a position inside the kraal and did not begin to trade until I was satisfied that I had enough stuff, carriers and containers, for the number of loads I intended to buy. Once I was satisfied, I posted an armed man at each gate and nobody was allowed to go outside. The remaining trooper and I did the trading, laid out the loads, collected the bearers and then immediately marched them off under escort.

I did have a little difficulty once again but I got over that. I made a miscalculation and found that I had three loads without bearers, and there were no males visible except the chief himself, a fine young native about 30 years of age, called 'Sodza,' who was sitting on a flat granite rock, surrounded by his old men – all ringed men. By searching I found two men hiding away. I went up to Sodza and asked him to get me another as I did not intend to lose face by having to leave one load behind. He told me he couldn't get one. I taunted him, saying: 'What, you the chief of a big village like this, and you cannot supply me with one man?' 'No,' he said. I told him that if he did not get me a man soon I would take him. His old councillors held up their hands in horror. He himself made no move, but just sat sulkily defying me. I lost patience and going into the circle I caught him by the arm and gave him the 'Policeman's Twist,' got him on his feet, and with the point of my revolver behind his ear, led him to the pack and made him pick it up. I took him over to where the rest of the convoy was waiting and handed him over, telling him what would happen to his village if any of the loads failed to reach their destination. The party moved off and all went well. I never saw Sodza again, but he carried his load and was duly rewarded.

We travelled from kraal to kraal, getting the goods and taking it in turns to escort the convoy into camp. On one occasion when I went into camp I found that a rifle had been damaged owing to it having been fired while the barrel was blocked with a cleaning rag. The muzzle had burst near the top. Getting the barrel cut down made the weapon quite a good-looking carbine, without any foresight of course. As it was useless to us I got permission to take it with me as a present for some chief. On our arrival at a big village I called on the chief and with due ceremony presented him with the carbine and a few rounds of ammunition as a token of goodwill. The old gentleman was thrilled to the marrow at this gift. We were immediately given the 'Freedom of the City,' as it were. A hut was cleaned out, new mats were put on the floor for us and shortly after we got in, a goat kid was sent with the chief's compliments. I must state that owing to the depredations of the Matabele which I have already mentioned, the amount of livestock possessed by these people was woefully small and the present of a goat kid was an act of great generosity. We borrowed an enormous earthenware pot, cut up the kid, and together with quantities of small tomatoes, which we had discovered at this place (goodness only knows where the original seeds came from), pumpkins and pink rice, we made a gorgeous stew and we four sat down to the best meal we had had since we left our homes. We only wished that our comrades in camp could have shared our banquet at this place.

We did excellently from a trading point of view as well and had no trouble at all. We were armed with Martini Henry rifles and our cartridges were solid drawn brass. I had tried using a few empty ones for barter and found that the women loved them. They made belts and anklets and used them in their dances – the jingling giving them great pleasure. These empty cartridge cases proved very useful in supplementing our trade goods, the stock of which was getting very low.

We saw at this kraal what I imagine was the trial of a woman for adultery. I am not of course sure about this, anyhow, a woman was accused of something and a jury of old men listened gravely to the evidence. After a long trial, a cord was bound round the woman's forehead and held at the other end by one woman, while other women, with light branches in their hands, hit the culprit, who was thus driven out of her home to another kraal some distance away. We understood that she was being taken back to her parents. The whole business was conducted with dignity and decorum and I very much regretted that my very limited knowledge of the language made it impossible to follow the proceedings closely.

Another interesting experience was to watch the village

blacksmith at work. An open fire on a granite rock, a charcoal fire, two complete skins of young goats with a piece of wood across the neck and wooden tubes at the bottom of the stomach – these were the principal gadgets. These tubes entered into a larger clay tube which went through a little clay door on to the fire. A man held each skin by the bit of wood across the neck and pressed each skin alternately. It was surprising to see how strong a blast this very quaint bellows produced. Meanwhile the craftsmen fashioned their hoes, battleaxes, knives, etc. Some miles away was a mountain called by the natives 'Thaba Insimbi' (iron mountain). From this the natives got the iron ore, smelted it into pig iron and then into the desired article. The finished result by this primitive method was remarkable.

The women make the string for basketmaking, game snares and other uses. A group get together and children peel the inner fibre from the bark of certain trees. The fibre is passed to the women who sit round and do all the rolling of it on their thighs, moistening the fibre from time to time with saliva. The speed with which they work is amazing and in a very little time they have long coils. This string is tremendously strong.

The women also are the potters. I regret that with the coming of civilisation most of the work described must have become a lost art. Some forty years after the time of which I am writing, I went with my son-in-law, who was a Government Medical Officer, to a large native reserve about 50 miles from Salisbury where he was investigating an outbreak of smallpox and I almost wept to see the difference from the unspoilt, unclothed, unsophisticated, cleanly natives of the past, to the present people clothed in dirty European clothes, and riding bicycles. I suppose civilisation has brought them benefits, but I liked the old order best. However, I must not moralize but get on with my story.

Another article which we traded for was 'Kaffir beer.' This was made from grain and was sometimes good, sometimes indifferent, and sometimes bad. It was, however, both food and drink, and many of our malaria patients convalesced on it.

Owing to excessive in-breeding, the native livestock was very small. Their cows and bulls were only the size of little donkeys and their fowls like bantams – eggs were not much bigger than pigeon eggs. Once when I had a noon-day halt, I sat by a fire on which I had placed a tin pannikin with water. As the water boiled, I broke an egg first to see if it was eatable. If so, I put it in the pannikin and poached it. In this way I broke 19 eggs, of which only nine were eatable. On another occasion I was riding with the dispatches and came to a post station which was in charge of a very good pal of mine, R. Carruthers Smith, and he got a meal ready for me which consisted of eight eggs. This sounds greedy, but was not so really.

On the whole our relations with the natives during the weeks we were collecting food were quite good. We had to be firm, but we never ill-treated any of them – always gave them a square deal and above all, never in the slightest way did we interfere with their womenfolk. I shall always be glad that I was privileged to go amongst these natives, see them at their daily tasks and marvel at their ingenuity. Altogether it was a most interesting and unforgettable experience. I forgot to mention earlier that before we introduced coarse salt to them, they satisfied their cravings for this essential by burning a kind of salt bush and using the ash as a substitute.

Another problem now presented itself – boots and clothes – we were like 'Falstaff's ragged army.' Some of the men had fashioned breeches out of the cheap cloth we had for trading purposes, and as for boots, they were practically *non est*. I have mounted in charge of the Main Guard at Fort Charter with myself in a pair of broken civilian boots which I had bought at a sale of the effects of a man who had died – one of my guard had on a pair of thick army socks – the rest were barefooted.

I was again sent for by Captain Turner, who told me that he had received information that the wagons bringing boots were held up at the Lundi River, the same river which had held us up. He instructed me to take ten donkeys which we had running about the camp, and to get the boots from the wagons. The Lundi was about 200 miles south of us. We had no pack saddles or gear of any kind, so, choosing as a companion Trooper Short, we started fashioning pack saddles. We got a number of large grain sacks and sewing up the open end, threw one over each donkey's back and then cut across the middle of the upper side. This gave us a pocket on either side. Then we made breast-straps, cinches and cruppers out of some cotton blankets and succeeded in making quite a good job of it one way and another, and feeling satisfied with our endeavours we set out.

We travelled fairly fast and made good progress. At night we made kraals of bush and penned the donkeys. We were a bit scared of lions, as donkeys are much favoured by these animals for food. Fortunately we were not troubled at all. One afternoon we came on some wagons outspanned and to our great joy found it was the convoy we were looking for – the Lundi River had gone down enough to enable them to get through, and they had come on as quickly as possible. The spot where we met was about 50 miles north of Fort Victoria. I had despatches with me for Victoria, so telling Short to get on with the transfer of the boots, I pushed on by myself. Just at dark I got to one of our despatch riding stations – Makowri.

This was in charge of my good pal R. Carruthers Smith (Jock) and he gave me a good meal. My horse was pretty tired and I wanted a change, as, of course, I had to go straight through. The only horse Jock could give me was a pony, light, and in not too good condition – so, to ride light, I left rifle, blankets and coat and rode in my shirt sleeves. It was summer and this was no hardship, but I had cause to regret that I had been foolish enough to leave my rifle and bandolier.

Makowri was about 40 miles from Victoria, so I could make it easily by early morning. About midnight, when I was jogging along at an easy canter I heard behind me the pad-pad of some animal in the road. I looked round and saw what I at first took to be a lion. I got the wind up properly and thought my number was up. I put spurs to the pony and tore down the road. After a while I pulled up a bit and shortly afterwards I heard the pad-pad – how I regretted the absence of my rifle. The animal came no nearer and I began to realise that it could not be a lion, so I just went slowly on, but the pad-pad behind me got on my nerves and I determined to try to end it. I stopped suddenly, pulled the pony around sharply and shouted loudly. The beast scurried off into the thick bush and I saw that it was a large hyena. As he disappeared I set off into the thick bush thinking that I had got rid of him, but after I had covered a couple of miles I again heard the pad-pad. Again from a canter I swung my pony quickly around, and taking off my big slouch hat, I charged down on the brute. I let out a tremendous yell and stooping over, almost hit him with the hat and he cleared again into the bush.

Just after this, to my very pleasant surprise, I came on a single wagon outspanned by the roadside. I roused the people and found that it was a prospecting party. I explained the position to them, telling them that I was carrying despatches and could not stay, but asked for a loan of a rifle and some ammunition. I told them I would be passing up again as I was returning as soon as I had delivered my letters at Fort Victoria and they would have the rifle back at least by late afternoon. After consultation among themselves they refused to lend me a rifle. Then I got nasty and told them that as we, the Police, were in possession of the country and anybody coming in at that stage was dependent on us, on my return I would pass the word along to all the police posts and between us we would give them such a hell of a time that they would be glad to get out of the country. I was making no idle boast and this they at last realised, and after another consultation very reluctantly handed me over a rifle and three cartridges! I thanked them and pushed off again, feeling much more comfortable.

My friend the hyena must have known that I was now armed, because I never saw nor heard him again and reached Fort Victoria without further incident. After having some breakfast, I managed to get seven fresh donkeys from the Officer Commanding – these were to help out our own ten – as I was in a hurry to get back to Fort Charter. I also wangled a fresh horse and started on my return journey driving my seven donkeys. It was some job till I got them settled down and I have every sympathy with the Irishman who has to drive a pig to market.

In due course I passed the prospectors' wagon, and returned the rifle and 3 cartridges. They told me that the hyena had stopped round their wagon for the rest of the night, howling his mournful tune and kept them awake. I was glad! Reaching Makowri I had a good meal (8 eggs), took over my own horse and pushed on to overtake Short. I found he had loaded his packs and had started back. He was very glad to see me and we found the extra donkeys most useful. We made good time and to our surprise met our troop on the road about 20 miles south of Fort Charter. We were most heartily welcomed by everybody from the Skipper down. It did not take long to distribute the boots and the men were as proud of their new boots as a woman with a 300 guinea fur coat.

I knew before I left Fort Charter that the troop was under orders to proceed east to the Portuguese Border where there was some trouble, but owing to the lack of footwear we could not move, so I was surprised to find the troop coming south. I was soon enlightened. The Transvaal Dutch had long cast covetous eyes on the country now known as Rhodesia, teeming as it was with game of all sorts, well wooded, well watered, with plenty of good arable land and ancient gold workings. The Matabele nation, however, were known to be great fighters and I think the Boers thought the risk a bit too great. This, however, is my own private opinion. However, Rhodes was prepared to take the risk with 750 men and so 'beat them to it.' When the Boers saw that we had made a bloodless conquest of the country over which they used to hunt without let or hindrance (we met one hunting party coming out with the hides of no less than 15 hippopotami on their wagons) they were very annoyed. A series of meetings were held in the Transvaal and a large 'trek' or 'commando' was organised with a man named Adendorff as leader and Col. Ferreira as military adviser.

South African history tells the wonderful story of the Dutch Voortrekkers (first travellers) who, dissatisfied with British rule in the old Cape Colony, principally in regard to the freeing of slaves, trekked with indomitable courage and limited resources into the unknown, to find a new country for themselves. They thus founded the Orange Free State and the Transvaal Republic, after suffering incredible hardships and encountering many bloody fights with Kaffirs – a parallel with the taming of the American West by the courageous frontiers-men. So that this threat to us by people with such a formidable record was not to be treated lightly and the news that this commando was advancing to take the country away from us and to declare a new Boer Republic created great excitement among our leaders and steps were immediately taken to resist this incursion with all our might – hence the hurried movements of the troops.

Here I must digress to tell of a fact which I have never seen mentioned, and which to my mind adds to the great personality of Rhodes. He must, at that time, have been greatly worried, yet before 'D' Troop moved on, the men were addressed by the O/C who read out a message from Rhodes. This set out the possibility of hard fighting and added that any Dutch South African, of whom we had a good number in the ranks, who had any scruples against fighting their countrymen, would be allowed to remain behind without any loss of rights whatsoever. To the credit of the troop, not one man fell out – they very properly argued that as we had taken the first risks we were entitled to hold what we had. I think this was a splendid gesture on the part of Rhodes. Had it been taken advantage of we would have lost the services of a number of our best men.

Our troop's objective was a place called 'Narka Pass,' a long way south of Fort Victoria. This was an opening in a long range of hills through which the Boers would have to come. Our artillery, a light gun firing a one-pound shell, and Maxim or Nordenfelt machine-guns, was posted on the hills to cover the entrance to the Pass. The men were kept busy, all bush for 1,000 yards in front of the post was cleared and ranges marked out, then we sat down to wait for an enemy who never turned up. Our first line of defence was at the crossing on the Crocodile River (this was the boundary dividing the Transvaal from Rhodesia). At this spot were concentrated the troops from Fort Tuli, our base depot. Forts of stout tree trunks and earthworks were hastily made and a couple of machine guns trained on the crossing.

The advance party of Boers, numbering some 200, reached the drift or crossing and announced their intention of continuing their journey. Dr Jameson, with an interpreter, went across the river and warned the leaders that their entry would be resisted (our force on the spot consisted of 140 men and two maxim guns) and advised them to retrace their steps. Col. Ferreira, their military adviser, also advised that the idea of forcing their way be abandoned. Sir Henry Loch, the Governor of the Cape Colony, had warned the Transvaal that the threat to Rhodesia would be taken seriously by the British Government. The Transvaal Government in turn had told the trekkers that the contemplated raid would not be countenanced by them and would be carried out at the trekkers' own risk. This accumulation of warnings gave Adendorff and Barend Vorster and their companions cause to consider and at a meeting held by them they decided to abandon the enterprise. So ended a situation which for a time looked very serious.

Now for the anti-climax. A number of the Boers sought and obtained permission to cross the river for the purposes of trade, and horses, meal and tobacco, etc., were disposed of. Col. Ferreira got permission to trek through the country and later I met him under peculiar circumstances, which I will describe later, at the Zimbabwe Ruins close to Fort Victoria.

To return to the march of 'D' Troop from Fort Charter to Narka Pass, on the last trek before reaching Fort Victoria I was left behind to look for lost horses. These I fortunately found and followed on. On the first trek out of Fort Victoria we camped for the night at Fern Spruit at the foot of Providential Pass, a lovely spot with a fast runing crystal-clear stream. Next morning at day break we started to inspan, when a whole span of oxen (16) was reported missing. Capt. Turner told me to remain behind and search for them together with a conductor. Capt. Turner left me his shooting horse, a fine upstanding salted bay, to ride. This was a valuable animal as it was immune from the dread scourge of horse sickness.

As soon as it was fully light we started off into the bush. After about three hours searching we were extremely lucky to come on the complete span some miles off the road and were soon on the way back. As I was riding along I saw a Riet buck – or rather, just his head, in the long grass. I would never have spotted him had I been on foot. I pulled up, dropped the reins and had a shot. He dropped, and on riding up I found I had hit him at the base of the skull and he had been killed instantly. My horse had not moved a muscle while I fired off his back. He was truly a shooting horse.

After doing the necessary with the buck, I fastened him behind the saddle. We reached the road at last and shortly after found a prospectors' wagon outspanned. We were very hungry by this time, so I bargained with the prospectors – half the buck for two good breakfasts. They were very glad to do this to get the fresh meat and we ate heartily. After travelling about seven or eight miles further we found the wagon belonging to the lost oxen at the roadside with Sergt.-Major Cunningham and several men. This wagon had been trailed behind another for the first morning trek and then dropped, to wait for us. The Skipper was very optimistic, as the chances of our finding the oxen in that thick bush were not too great. The Sergt.-Major and his companion would have had a thin time had we not turned up. We handed over horses and cattle to the native herd boy while we rested.

At 4 p.m. the Sergt.-Major ordered inspan – the oxen were brought in, when it was found that the two horses were missing – the herd boy could give no explanation. All hands went out, but no trace of the animals could be found. The Sergt.-Major decided to move on with the wagon and ordered me to remain behind to find the horses. I could not refuse, of course, but protested that it was jolly rough to be left at the roadside by myself. The Sergt.-Major said he would not order another man to stay, but if one of the other troopers volunteered to stay with me, he would raise no objection. At this, Trooper R. Carruthers Smith, the youngest amongst them, stepped forward and said he would stay. I could not have had a better half-section. Though younger than I was, Jock, as we all called him, had already tried farming in Canada and was well able to take care of himself. The Sergt.-Major doled us out a few days' rations and then pushed off, and it was not until the wagon had been gone some time that I discovered that my half buck which I had carried so far had also gone on with it, so we were without any fresh meat.

For some days we searched the surrounding country, one of us seeking while the other stayed with our kit. Our nights were greatly disturbed by the barking of wild dogs. Fortunately there was plenty of firewood so we had a good blaze all night. About the fourth day some natives passed by, one had a basket of eggs, which we promptly traded for, so securing a much-needed change of diet.

One morning when I was busy poaching an egg in a tin pannikin some horsemen appeared. I stood up and found it was the Officer Commanding, Col. Pennefather, who was on his way down country, inspecting his troops. I stood to attention, with my pannikin containing an egg in one hand and a fork in the other! 'What on earth are you men doing here?' he asked. 'Looking for lost horses, Sir,' I replied. At this he let himself go and I got such a telling-off – it was no good telling him that I had not lost the horses, so I just suffered in silence. He said we were not to be trusted with goats, let alone such valuable animals as horses. When the Colonel had completely exhausted his vocabulary he rode off. I looked round speechlessly at Jock, who was standing behind me and found him helpless with laughter. He had not had the 'telling-off' – I, as corporal, got it all.

One day as I was out a long way from the road I came on the spoor of a lioness and two cubs in the bed of a sandy river. As I was looking for horses, not lions, I turned back. At length we saw some more natives and told them what we were after and promised a blanket for each horse if found. This was a wonderful reward to them and soon a large number of boys were out searching – personally, Jock and I were done. We had just about finished our food, we had not seen any game in our searching around, so I decided to move on. I knew that the Tokwe River was only about 7 or 8 miles away and I was almost sure to find someone outspanned there. Packing ourselves with saddles, bridles, rifles, bandoliers with ammunition, blankets and various belongings, we started off. We did about 6 miles when lack of food told its tale and poor Jock was beat and could not continue. I was getting anxious when fortunately a native happened to come along. I commandeered him and he shouldered Jock's load and we set off again. Reaching the river I was delighted to find a wagon outspanned, proving that my hunch was right. We asked for food, which was given us. After a meal we both felt much better and happier.

During the night we were awakened by the noise of a convoy crossing the river at a drift about 200 yards higher up. I turned out and found that these were the transports that had taken our troops down to Narka Pass and were now returning to Fort Victoria. To my relief the man in charge told me he had brought a week's rations for the two of us, so with easy minds we turned in again and had a good night's rest.

On the 12th day after we had been dropped, to our great joy two natives turned up, each leading a horse. The animals were in good shape as the grazing was good. We immediately tied them up securely and except for taking them to water, never loosed them till we saddled up to resume our journey. We gladly handed over a blanket to each of the natives to their great joy — the first they had ever possessed. I can imagine what a sensation they caused when they returned to their kraals.

That night we got up in turn to see that the horses were still there! Next morning bright and early we packed our saddles and mounted, feeling real good, and started off and rejoined the Troop without further incident. Captain Turner was very pleased to see us and also the horses — so pleased was he, in fact, that soon after I got into my tent the officers' mess waiter came up and presented me with the Captain's compliments and a bottle of whisky. Whisky to the troops was worth its weight in gold, but as for myself, I did not take liquor in those days. However, the news soon spread and lots of the chaps came round to welcome me back! I had a small tin which was used for our pea-meal ration and everyone who came along was given it filled with a small measure of whisky — I was never so popular in all my life!

The man with whom I shared a tent was called Eksteen, a Dutch South African, and one of the best. Poor Billy had a bad attack of lumbago and I found him suffering great pain. I went to the doctor and asked him to give me something to relieve

Eksteen. The only thing he could give me was a mustard leaf.

I half-filled a tin pannikin with whisky, made Billy drink it, clapped on the leaf and covered him up well and soon he dropped off to sleep. Next morning he was still asleep and about 9 a.m. I began to get anxious and had an idea that as he had not had any liquor for so long he might be suffering from alcoholic poisoning. However, at about 10 a.m. he stirred. I asked him how the lumbago was. He said the pain of the lumbago had quite gone, but he felt a burning sensation where I had put the leaf. I took it off and it certainly did look as if that part had been burned. I had not known at the time that a mustard leaf should not be left on for more than 20 minutes! However, I cured Billy Eksteen of his lumbago.

Corporals' Mess, 'E' Troop, B.S.A.C. Police, Macloutsie Camp, 1890
Left to right (standing): W. Block (cook), J. Goldsbury, H. Butler, J. Cardew
Front (sitting): F. Fitzgerald, E. Finucane, C.H. Divine, H.T. Knight, E.A. Farmery

1900s

THE CAMELIRO

George Henry 'Hacker' Matthews
Trooper No. 523, British South Africa Police

An episode has just come back vividly to me through the medium of a dream, and I would like your readers to have the facts of the only command I ever held, other than O.C. Kitchen, whilst I was in the B.S.A. Police. CAMELS! Ye Gods! Little wonder I sometimes dream of 'em, but that is a detail compared to what some of the characters set down herein must have endured. Nightmares at the very least. My title must be taken with a grain of salt but I have in mind Spanish bull-fights, so the word may suit the occasion.

Before I carry on, I might say in American film poster parlance that a man in charge of camels should be a right, rollicking, rough he-man with a hangman's propensities and a lion-taming, boxing-booth commissionaire training experience of at least 25 years.

It was about 1905, when the late Lieut.-Col. Chester Masters, Commandant, B.S.A. Police, arrived in the Sinoia Camp with eleven camels and established a riding school. The Exhibition rodeo simply couldn't possibly come into the same street with that riding school, and I believe that some of the boys down for leave must have cancelled their sea trip. They all joined up with the exception of Sgt.-Major McMillan, who refused point blank 'tae have onything tae do wi' the beasts'. After three days' riding on the billowy briney, the Colonel announced his intention of returning to Salisbury, and called for a man to proceed with him for a course of camels. When the 'one pace forward' order came along, I beat 'Yappy' Smith by inches, but should really have been disqualified for crossing, boring and bumping. I ask you, who wouldn't have made a dirty dive for that job, carrying as it did 2s. 6d. per day E.D.P., with a native assistant chucked in? Cushy! That's the word.

After a five-day uneventful voyage I arrived in Salisbury with my charge and took up my quarters at the Transport Camp under the name of 'Cameliro George'. I was issued with Col.

Flint's book on how to 'treat' camels, and at the end of two months (most of which time I spent down Pioneer Street, where if the truth must be known, there were no camels), I was doled out with; Camels, 3; riding saddles, 2; pack saddle, 1; native, 1 (according to ritual), and then the band really struck up.

My instructions were to proceed back to my station, Sinoia, and we cast our mooring, and I can tell you it wasn't only the camels who had the hump. My first off-saddle was Mount Hampden (possibly because I was a bona fide traveller for a drink, there being a hotel there at that time), and the rest of the journey went off without anything specially exciting taking place other than camel No. 2 taking a personal dislike to my native assistant. I was just in time to prevent a recurrence of the Gotch-Hackenschmidt bout, for my boy was almost on the mat.

On the evening of the fifth day out I arrived at Sinoia and it was a beautiful evening – stables were in progress, the men were grooming the horses and the natives the mules when I appeared in the clearing and surveyed the serenity of an out-station in the peaceful calm of sundown. I heard old 'Mac' (Sgt.-Major McMillan) come out with that time-honoured 'Now then! Stop that talking and put some life into it,' but not a soul dreamt of the terrible blow which was about to fall on this little out-of-the-way spot.

I think it was Major Addison's horse *Birton* which first winded the camels. He lifted his head and snorted, and in less than a minute the men stood with curry-comb and brush in hand with nothing to use 'em on. There were about thirty animals, and they cleared hell-for-leather into the veld, when the S.M. suddenly became aware of my presence and he strutted over to me in high dudgeon. What he didn't say to me never was, the mildest sentence placing 'Cameliro' George and his menagerie out of bounds.

If it hadn't been for that 2s. 6p. E.D.P. I might also have been excluded from the canteen bust-up, but after a while I got on the right side of the S.M., and one night we made up a party about twelve strong and proceeded by camel to Deary's store on the Eldorado side of the Hunyani River. Gee whizz! That was some party and being in a convivial mood there was every excuse for a 'quite well, thank you' state of affairs being palpable when we commenced the return journey, transforming each camel into a Handley Page with five passengers. We got nicely into the drift, which was running three feet high, when the leading camel (appropriately named Page), with the S.M. as part of its human freight, got a bit weary.

The S.M. said to his mount, 'hush' (get down) instead of 'hut' (get a move on) and the camel immediately did the needful by getting down to it, with the result that the two followers came up, thanked the leader kindly and joined him in the rippling brook.

We all had to subtract ourselves from those blankety camels before they would deign to rise, and everything went well until that blasted leader took a notion to make a short cut, and we next got mixed up with the barbed wire surrounding the cemetery. We were subsequently forced to finish our return journey on foot, the camels having developed a liver. Sgt. George Michie and 'Yappy' Smith each got a kick on the clock and they likened it to a slap with a sack of soft mealie pap.

Some time after, I was ordered to convey one Tpr. Alex Goodlet to Hartley to open up the Gatooma station. When we arrived at the Giant Mine they had just dropped the stamps and were celebrating the occasion at the local club. I said to Alex, 'This looks as if I'll have to sing a song for a drink.' So we put the camels down on the darkest side of the club (it was night) and strolled in amongst the boys. There was an immediate shout of 'Come on, Hacker, give us a song,' and after two or three I.I.s and soda I got busy, and we were in, boots an' all. Everything went swimmingly until a couple of chaps had to go out for some reason or other and got too close to one of the camels which didn't argue.

Oh no! He merely advertised his presence giving voice to a gurgling grunt. These two guys were back in the club without having let their feet touch the ground. They called for guns, which were forthcoming, together with lamps, to make short work of the lion or lions which had the temerity to come right slap-bang up against the club. I was in the middle of one of my favourites, saw the disturbance at the back and was just in time to save those Egyptians from a hasty exit. Next day we journeyed into Hartley and arrived there about 4.30 p.m., fixing the camels in the bush behind the stables. I then got down to it, not feeling too good after the night before. My slumbers were short-lived for Sgt. Young came along and said, 'Come on, you chaps, and get these horses and mules in.' But believe me, those horses and mules had made up their minds not to be at home to anyone. Sgt. Young and Cpl. Simpson went right off the deep end with the men and natives the next morning, so I thought it propitious to stroll up casually and say, 'I wonder if the camels have put the breeze up your stable; I think I'll shift them further down the road,' which I did and everything in the garden righted itself.

Needless to say, for the second time I was placed out of bounds (with my luggage), this time by Captain 'Jimmie' Tait. My suite was a curiosity in that dorp, and I clicked with the seaside penny-a-ride-on-the-donkey's-back stunt, but I shan't tell you what my fee was. Later on a very untoward occurrence cropped up by the boss camel falling sick. My native attendant came along and said, '*Lo squesa* (camel) *ikona hamba bush*,' so I reported the matter to Captain Tait and informed him that I had come to the conclusion that half a gallon of linseed oil was necessary to get this machine to earn me futi remuneration on the beach stunt.

It is the easiest thing in the world to give a camel medicine; You simply get him down in the usual position, tie his legs, pass a looped rope over his upper jaw, pull his head back over his hump, and there you are. There is no escape and the dope runs down his neck like dirty water down a drain pipe, with very much the same sound. The half-gallon of linseed oil had no effect, and as I posed as an authority on camels, the eyes of the camp were on me. It was a case of kill or cure, and as Col. Flint seemed to have stopped short in his treatise there was nothing left but my imagination. The 'Cameliro' then requisitioned 7lb Epsom salts which he mixed up in a bucket of warm water (about five gallons). In passing I might say that I didn't like my name then.

We got the funnel from the top of a near-by mealie grinding machine and yanked the stuff down the camel's neck to the accompaniment of, 'Be careful, Matthews, don't overdo it' from Captain Tait. My reply, as near as I can remember, was, 'That's all right, sir, the water goes straight to his hump in case of a dry season, and the salts to his pantry.' As everyone knows, a camel has a very intelligent and human look in his eyes and this one was no exception to the rule. He gazed at me and seemed to say, 'Ch...t, Hacker, have a heart.' Anyway, after waiting a reasonable time we gave him half a dozen No. 9 horse pills which had been struck off the strength two years before, and finished up with 2lb of jallop, with the result that he chucked a seven next morning. At the post-mortem we found the trouble to be a length of barbed wire which had got mixed up with his last three meals, so the onus was removed from my shoulders. What narks me is the fact that I should have used blasting powder instead of the usual methods.

Sgt. Young gave the natives orders to bury that camel, but the Maswinas would have nothing to do with it. You see, camels in that dorp had the Indian sign on them. I suggested cremation, whereupon we stacked wood round the carcass and fired up. 'H—l! I can still smell that camel roasting.' Capt. 'Jimmie' Tait said, 'Matthews, you had better hit the trail, for if another of those ruddy camels picks this camp out for a final resting place, we shan't have any men, horses or boys left; It will bewitch the pitch for good.'

I have just heard casually from Major Brereton that a male member of my circus was subsequently at Tuli in 1915, attached to the Police for patrol duty. He was a damned nuisance, possibly due to his harem being discontinued.

The Major wasn't too communicative and I couldn't get any more out of him, but I've an idea that camel died.

Camel at Gwanda 1906

Camels at Gwanda 1910

1910s

The MAZUNGA PATROL of September 1918

Herbert Frederick Montagu Surgey
Trooper No.1860, British South Africa Police

Your Editor, having unearthed an old field message book (Army Book 153), noticed my name recorded in it as a member of the Advance Party Scouting Screen for the main body on the Mazunga Patrol. The writings of the late Lieutenant Bridger, written mainly on both sides of each page in indelible pencil, having become very faint with the passage of time, I have been asked to help in filling in some of the illegible portions to provide an account of an event which may have some historical value but which is certainly of interest in the light of the passing of fifty years.

It is unfortunate that only the daily time-table portions can be deciphered with any ease. Lieutenant Bridger's reports to the Officer Commanding, the late Major Georgie Stops, can be read in parts before fading out almost completely. The time-table, however, is of great assistance to me in recalling the incidents of the Patrol from the angle of a 25-year-old Trooper with just under five years of police service to his credit.

As one gets older, it seems to be a biological fact that incidents of one's youth, for one reason or another, remain fresher in the memory than more recent happenings. To make the Patrol into any sort of story, I have freely made use of that which can be deciphered from Lieutenant Bridger's writings – and have then added my recollections to fill in the gaps.

Mazunga, in the West Nicholson area of the Gwanda District, contained a small settlement of Europeans and was also the headquarters of Liebig's Ranching Company. In 1918, a Mr MacKenzie was the Ranch Manager and he had under his control a number of Europeans employed as Section Managers and Dip Tank Supervisors. The homes of these employees were widely scattered throughout this huge area of dry bush-veld ranching country. They were inter-connected by private dirt roads suitable for animal-drawn transport and a single wire-earth-return private telephone system. The line was carried on insulators attached to the higher branches of mopani trees. As one might expect, there were times when the lines were out of action. Giraffe and elephant were numerous and had little respect for the frail wires of communication – to say nothing of the native tenants of the ranch who found many uses for the copper wire strung so casually across the veld.

It is recorded that towards the end of August 1918 a scared-looking native arrived at one of the Section Managers' houses and told a very unlikely-sounding story. He said that portions of the Shangaan Tribe living under Chief Sengwa near Pafuri at the southern end of the Rhodesian-Portuguese border, were in a state of unrest and had murdered several European labour recruiters – the only Europeans known to be living in that remote area. The informant had heard that the next move on the part of the tribesmen was to be a raid on the nearest European settlements or farms with the object of stealing arms and cattle. The date set for the raid was the first full moon in September.

The information was passed on to the Native Commissioner at Chibi, Mr Hemans, who intimated that he had absolutely no confirmation of the alleged murders or of any tribal unrest. The management of Liebig's took no comfort from the Native Commissioner's assessment. They lost no time in bringing certain people into laager and posting guards from the Mazunga Rifle Platoon at strong points, on store buildings and water supplies. Having done this, the manager then called for police assistance. Because of Pafuri's isolation and complete lack of telephonic communications, there was only one way to test the accuracy of the informant's startling information.

It was decided to send a strong patrol from Bulawayo, commanded by Major Stops and with Lieutenant Bridger as his second-in-command.

September 6 1918
Entrain and out of Bulawayo 11.30 a.m. Arrive West Nicholson 8 p.m. Orders issued 11 p.m.

We were met on arrival at West Nicholson by Major Stops in his privately-owned Hupmobile car. An advance party was selected for the scouting screen as follows:

Lieutenant J.S. Bridger (Horse 1041 Lancer).
Sergeant R. Jones (Horse 872 Jack).
Farrier Trooper S. Jacobs (Horse 927).
Troopers: H.M. Surgey (Horse 081 Khaki). S.D. Truscott

(Horse 1043). E.V. Deane (Horse 097). R.J. Howe (Horse remount).

Transport: Buckboard and 8 mules; one pack mule; driver and leader; one Native Constable Orderly and bicycle; one Native Constable, Officer's batman.

After we had sorted ourselves out, camp was made in the Railway Station shunting yards – most uncomfortable but at least handy for the early start the next morning.

The main body, who had been detailed for the unloading, made camp near a pool of the Umzingwane River at a site prepared by the thoughtful NCO in charge at West Nicholson, Corporal 'Tickey' Edwards. He and his detachment had thought of everything. Picket lines had been set up for the animals, hay had been supplied, camp fires were burning brightly and water was on the boil. We all said a big 'thank-you' to 'Tickey' and his men.

September 7 1918

9.30 a.m. Left West Nicholson with the advance party. Arrived Becker's Farm 1.15 p.m. Moved out at 4 p.m. and arrived Mtshabesi River 6 p.m. Mileage 27.

At about 10 a.m., who should we see approaching us but the mounted figure of Trooper Hockley, on his way back to West Nicholson from a patrol somewhere in the Mazunga direction. I can't remember if our mission was a complete surprise to him or if he had been sent off prior to our arrival to spy out the land and confirm the rumour of Shangaan unrest. I do remember this, however. From his point of view we were engaged on a wild goose chase. George reckoned that if there had been any unrest, it would have been impossible to keep the matter secret. When we arrived at Becker's farm, a question arose. Who was to be the party's cook? Someone (bless him) remembered that the late Charlie Rogers and I had been cooks for Sergeant Harry Onyett's Number 2 Troop on the Sesheke Column of 1915. As Charlie was not with our party, I was elected and it fell to my lot to attend to the cooking with Eric Venables Deane to handle the bread making. He was an expert and turned out some excellent bread using only a bake pan. I seemed to get by – as a cook – since no one tried to assault me during the trip. There was an advantage in the detail in that I was excused grazing and night guards – as I had to start the breakfast well before Reveille.

September 8 1918

Reveille 1.30 a.m. Moved off at 2.30 a.m. and arrived at Mikados Outspan at 6.15 a.m. Moved off again at 10.30 a.m. and arrived at Section III Dip Tank at 2 p.m. Moved out at 3.45 p.m. and arrived at Mazunga at 5.30 p.m. Mileage 41.

On arrival at Mazunga we were challenged by a sentry posted on a drift by the Officer Commanding the Mazunga Rifle Platoon. We gathered from the sentry that some of the outlying families had come into laager – just in case – and that water supplies and stores were being guarded during the hours of darkness by members of the Rifle Platoon. Their leader came up, gave us a hearty welcome, and informed us that now he could hand over all the guard duties to us! Much to his surprise, Lieutenant Bridger begged to differ and told the O.C. Rifle Platoon that we had our hands full with grooming and stable picquet that night. He told him that Major Stops would be arriving on the morrow with the full party and that suitable arrangements could then be made about the guard duties.

We made a trip to Jaffe's General Dealers' Stores and bought tins of Van Houten's cocoa so that we could brew up commidges of 'bergoo' in our billy cans when on guard duty.

September 9 and 10 1918

Stables 6 a.m. Cleaning up ~ writing wires in code all morning. Rested in the afternoon. Left camp at 8.40 p.m. with same details as before and trekked until 12.10 a.m. Moved out again at 4.45 a.m. and arrived at Lamula's at 7 a.m. on September 10.

Spoke to Section Manager Johnson re news, but nothing fresh. Conversed with Major Stops on the phone 10 a.m. to 10.10 a.m. Outspanned until 3 p.m. Moved off at 5 p.m. and arrived at Bubye Dip Tank at 9 p.m.

Trooper Howe sick with sunstroke. Gave him salts and quinine. Temperature 101.5. Met Mr Hewett in charge of the Dip. No fresh news. Arranged with him for supply of mealies for animals. Guard mounted at midnight. Mileage 24.

Major Stops and the main body reached Mazunga at 5 p.m. on September 9. When we looked for our kit bags we were told that they had been loaded on to one of Liebig's ox-drawn scotch-carts and that the driver and leader had lost the oxen when they had been outspanned at Mikados. They had got drunk, of course! We were informed that as soon as our kit – containing such items as spare riding breeches, slacks, shorts, shirts, singlets etc., most necessary items on an extended patrol – arrived, it would be sent on to us. Our kit never arrived – the kitbags were sent back to West Nicholson.

All this time, it must be remembered, we had been travelling in Mobilization Order Mounted. Our only spare kit was in our wallets and the loss of our kitbags was something we had never anticipated. We couldn't wait for clean clothes (just as well as it turned out) and we left Mazunga as stated and trekked through the night.

September 11 1918
Reveille 5 a.m. Moved off at 6.15 a.m. and arrived at Natala's Well at 7.45 a.m. Called at Futumani's Kraal at 8.15 a.m. and brought him back to camp. I think he is genuinely not against the Government. I believe him when he says that he has no knowledge of the alleged murders of white men on the border.

Moved off at 3.40 p.m. and arrived at Lutopi Pools on the Bubye River at 5.55 p.m. Outspanned for the night. Mileage 15.

The diary goes on in this strain, day by day until September 20 when we returned to West Nicholson.

Farrier Trooper Jacobs was in charge of the buckboard on its trips back and forth to Mazunga for supplies. Camp was moved from place to place down the Bubye River towards the Portuguese Border and we would strike out in pairs to visit any kraals we knew of in the hope of gaining some information on the 'troubles'. None was forthcoming. All the Africans we saw were friendly and each and every one of them denied knowing anything of any murders at Pafuri or elsewhere on the border.

Finally a cyclist orderly arrived from Mazunga with instructions from Major Stops that we were to return to Mazunga as quickly as possible and that Lieutenant Bridger was to take command of the whole body and return to West Nicholson and Bulawayo.

We retraced our steps rapidly and, on reaching Mazunga, learned that Sergeant 'Mouldy' Duncombe had already left for West Nicholson and was one trek ahead of us. We tried to make up the interval but never did.

We were a tired and filthy mob when we eventually crossed the Umzingwane River on our way to that comfortable outspan in the Railway yards at about 6.30 a.m. Our appearance raised a big laugh and a cheer from the members of the main body who were having breakfast on the shady banks of the river. Shaved and smiling with a good night's rest behind them, they were certainly superior to the unkempt half-dozen of the scouting party.

After rubbing our horses down and seeing that feed was supplied to our mounts by the local West Nicholson detachment, we sought permission to have breakfast at the Hotel. This was approved but before we left, we were informed of the parades that had been laid on for the whole patrol: 9.30 a.m. Stables; 10.45 a.m. Arms Inspection; 11.30 a.m. Stripped Saddle Inspection.

We were not exactly overjoyed at the tidings.

When we arrived at the Hotel, to our great surprise and satisfaction we found that our kitbags had preceded us. 'Tickey' Edwards had seen to this and besides the clean but crumpled kit, he had also ordered hot baths to be waiting for us. He thought we might be needing them and how right he was. We engaged rooms at the Hotel and tumbled into bed in pyjamas between cool clean sheets.

The next thing I remembered was being shaken by Sergeant Jones who politely informed me that I was 'on the peg' for not being on evening stable parade which had just been dismissed and that into the bargain, our absence had been noted from morning stables, arms inspection and stripped saddle inspec-ion. We were all on a charge, all five troopers of the Advance Party.

We were not unduly worried. On the credit side we had all enjoyed about seven hours of solid undisturbed sleep and, above all, we felt clean for the first time in weeks.

Readers may wonder why, during the patrol, we rose so early, trekked by night when there was sufficient moon for us to see where we were going, and why we outspanned so often during the day. The answer is that we were travelling through dry and shadeless country at the hottest time of the year. Progress was best made when the sun was not fiercely beating down on man and beast. Our halts were made wherever there was some sort of rough grazing. The animals had to have roughage to keep some semblance of condition in the trying circumstances. During these halts there was little rest for us humans. We had to be continually moving our blankets around the stunted bushes or mopani trees to take full advantage of any shifting patches of shade.

What of the fitness of the scouting party? Lieutenant Bridger had a few rotten spells as did Trooper Howe, but both 'kept going' – there was no alternative. Most of us had spells of low fever-malaria – but that was normal in those days and none of us thought anything of it.

The return journey to Bulawayo from West Nicholson started on September 21, some of us going by rail and the rest by road via the Matopo Hills and Fort Usher police station.

One question which will be asked, by all policemen readers at any rate, is what happened to our native informant to whom we were indebted for the 'experience' of the excursion; that conveyor of glad tidings who sparked off the whole patrol. After being taken to Liebig's headquarters for questioning, he appears to have slipped away into obscurity. We never caught sight of him and had we had such good fortune, we would have had much pleasure in rewarding him for his troubles ... with a kick in the seat of his pants.

The saddest part of these memories for me is that all my comrades of the scouting party are dead. Someday, perhaps, I shall hear them whistling to me from the other side of the wall to jump over and join them. Only then will we be able to share the rest of our memories.

Note:
Trooper Surgey (H.M.S.) later became a Lieutenant-Colonel and Deputy Commissioner of the B.S.A.P.

1920s

PRELUDE to a LEGAL LIFE

My Five Years in the British South Africa Police
Roger Cazalet
Trooper 2526, British South Africa Police

Roger Cazalet served five years in the B.S.A.P., leaving to take up a legal career. He qualified as an Attorney and later founded his own Practice in Salisbury. He wrote his memoirs, entitled:

The Law – A Life Career which were never published

The story of his Police years was Part One of those Memoirs.

CONTENTS

Introduction by the Author

I was born at Brecon, Wales, on 11 October, 1902, and spent the early years of my life at my parents' home at Craddock, a small country hamlet in Devon between Uffculme and Culmstock, a few miles from Tiverton and the 'Lorna Doone' country.

I was subsequently educated at Copthorne, a preparatory school on the borders of Sussex and Surrey, not far from East Grinstead, and thereafter at Repton, which I left at the end of 1921. I was originally destined for the Royal Navy via Osborne and Dartmouth – more or less a family tradition – but Providence advisedly willed otherwise. The word 'advisedly' is relevant – the writer being one of the world's worst sailors (from a seasickness point of view).

It was hoped on leaving Repton I would proceed to Pembroke College, Cambridge, where my father had been previously, and thereafter to the Bar, but this was not to happen either, owing to the rapid decline in the family fortunes caused by the confiscation of the family estates and businesses in Russia at the end of the first world war (*Note below*). In the end result, partly for health reasons, I emigrated to South Africa in April, 1922, ostensibly to learn citrus growing at White River in the Eastern Transvaal.

At the end of a year it was equally clear, both to myself and to the Company which employed me, that citrus growing was not my metier – to put it mildly! Having now attained the ripe old age of 20 I was eligible to join the B.S.A.P., and through the kindness of an elderly cousin, Captain Alexander P.I. Cazalet, who had originally served in the B.B.P. and thereafter for many years in the B.S.A.P. in the early days and who had since retired to White River, it was arranged that provided I paid my rail fare to Salisbury and passed the medical examination on arrival, I would be enlisted.

Note: The Cazalet family of French origin hailed from the Pyrenees but being Huguenots (Protestants) were driven out of France as a result of the revocation of the Edict of Nantes by Louis XIV circa 1685 and, being dispossessed of their titles and estates, fled to England. My great, great, great paternal grandmother was a personal friend of Catherine II, Empress of Russia and it was as a result of this friendship that the Cazalet family obtained their estates and businesses in Russia. The name Cazalet is derived from two Latin words, 'Casa' and 'Letu'.

Incidentally, 'Mount Cazalet' and the Hotel at Gwanda are named after the said cousin, affectionately known as 'Pa' Cazalet throughout the Regiment, who for many years was Superintendent of Police i/c Gwanda District.

Rumour, a fickle jade at the best of times, has it that the reason for naming the kopje after him was because, renowned for his keenness on physical fitness, he made his troopers run up the kopje daily before breakfast – doubtless, and not without justification, they considered him somewhat overkeen.

History does not relate why the Hotel was named after him but, whatever the reason it was a gracious tribute to a highly esteemed old member of that world-renowned police force.

('Pa' Cazalet also served in the Matabeleland Mounted Police, during which period he took part in the Jameson Raid and was taken prisoner – he was later repatriated in the care of the Rev. R.M. Cazalet, of Truro, Cornwall. He was born in St Petersburg in 1855 and died in the late 1920s).

I am ashamed to confess that after fifty years in Rhodesia I have not, as yet, had the opportunity of visiting Gwanda and drinking to my cousin's memory – in situ, so to speak – but hope this sin of omission may be rectified before it is too late. It is unlikely I will have the chance of complying with the old adage 'See Naples and die', so more realistically, if not aesthetically, I had better lower my sights and be content to 'See Mount Cazalet and die!'

To resume; Having approached the Managing Director of the White River Estate Company, Mr Merriman, son of Percy X. Merriman, I tactfully sought and obtained his kind permission to be released from my contract in order to join the B.S.A. Police. Having parted on most amicable terms from my employers, but with a scarcely veiled sigh of relief on both sides and, moreover, having literally wiped the dust of White River from off my feet, I set forth for Southern Rhodesia and Salisbury where I arrived on a Sunday evening towards the end of April, 1923, shortly after the Country had decided, by referendum, to stand on her own feet and accept Responsible Government.

I little dreamt that Southern Rhodesia – to which country I completely lost my heart from the time I crossed her borders – was to become my permanent home and in view of my legal career starting with my joining the B.S.A.P., this will be a convenient place to end this introduction.

CHAPTER ONE
A Young Recruit in Depot

Having passed the medical examination I was attested into the B.S.A. Police (Regimental Number 2526).

The only person I knew in Southern Rhodesia at that time was Captain New (invariably known as 'Skipper' New) who, having resigned from the B.S.A. Police several years ago, now worked and lived in Salisbury. He proved a real friend to a young recruit in a strange land.

At the beginning of the century, when on long leave from the Police, 'Skipper' New used to stay at 'Craddock' with his brother, a landed proprietor from whom my parents leased their home 'Craddock Gleeve' immediately opposite – incidentally he used to push his niece and me about in the same pram. The entrance hall at 'Craddock' was adorned with a magnificent array of big game horns and trophies shot by 'Skipper' New while in the Police, which never ceased to fascinate me as I grew older, and aroused my keen interest in Southern Rhodesia from an early age.

'Skipper' New, a most genial and well-beloved character, will probably be best remembered as M.F.H of the Salisbury Fox Hounds until their disbandment, and latterly as 'Mine Host' for several years at Rhodes Hotel, Inyanga – on Christmas Day it was traditional for him to usher in the boar's head with a fanfare from his hunting horn which he blew with much skill and enthusiasm. He was very fond of children, by whom, including my own, he was dearly loved. I was allowed to visit him at the Rusape Hospital for a few minutes the day before he died, just to say a last fond farewell and God Speed, but he was in a deep sleep at the time from which he never awakened – may he rest in peace – bless him.

I will not weary the reader with undue details of the recruit course, which followed the pattern of all similar establishments, and consisted mainly of riding school, stables (grooming and watering horses) twice daily, mounted infantry drill, foot and musketry drill, rifle and revolver practice at the range and at 'Gun Kopje', guard duties at night in the guardroom and at the stables, to say nothing of the endless 'spit and polish' including all items of saddlery, as also daily lectures on horse management and equitation, Law and Police duties, First Aid and other subjects.

It must be remembered that at this time, and for several years to come, the B.S.A.P. carried out two main functions – primarily that of a Police Force and secondly that of the first line of defence for Southern Rhodesia which latter required additional training as Mounted Infantryman in sundry close-knit military formations complete with service rifle, bandolier and rifle bucket, which latter was suspended from the saddle.

I can think of no more nerve-wracking, frustrating or exhausting task than to endeavour to control with one hand a horse – fresh out of the stable and literally champing at the bit – on the early morning ride on a cold frosty winter morning, with the other hand being engaged in holding a rifle in the required position. To permit one's horse to tread on the heels of the horse in front was reckoned to be one of the deadly sins of commission and, though not punishable by death, heaven help the unfortunate recruit who sinned in this manner. It would be better for him were he not born!

After passing-out of the riding school stage the recruits' junior ride was taken by the R.S.M., Mr Douglas, late of the 'Scots Greys', affectionately known throughout the Force as 'Jock' but always addressed to his face as 'Sir' and as Mr Douglas by the officers. The R.S.M. rode a magnificent steed of great stature, the former being of no light weight, called S.O.B. (in view of the indelicate meaning of the first initial the true interpretation had better be left to the ingenuity of the reader). This horse was equally fresh and skittish on occasions and – 'Tell it not in Gath' – sometimes got out of control and when the Troop was proceeding at the customary walk-march, three commands would then be given in one breath – Trot, Canter, Gallop. This would result in hell being let loose and utter chaos would result with the horses, taking full advantage of this heaven sent opportunity, careering madly in all directions over the veld with rifles scattered in their wake. When eventually order was restored and formation resumed, the R.S.M. would tell us in no uncertain terms exactly what he thought of us and of our standard of equitation or rather the lack of it.

On one occasion when the troop was assembled in front of the stables prior to the early morning ride, I found myself without my horse 'Ginger', the latter for some reason or other having been removed from the stable without my knowledge. On the command being given by the R.S.M. – 'Stand to your horses – prepare to mount – get mounted' – I plucked up sufficient courage to call out, 'Please Sir, I have not got a horse,' which evoked the somewhat unexpected retort in a stentorian voice – 'I don't care – get mounted'!!The troop moved off leaving a somewhat dejected and forlorn recruit standing alone, 'silent upon a peak in Darien'.

Sport formed an important part of a recruit's training including cricket, tennis, boxing competitions, hockey, soccer and rugger – the three latter being played on hard grounds in those days – the resultant sores and gravel rashes had to be seen to be believed!

Cricket was played on a matting pitch. I well remember the jubilation when the Police hockey team, of which I happened to be one of the decidedly weaker players, defeated the main Salisbury team which had been 'Cock of the walk' for many seasons.

In those days a trooper's commencing pay, as a recruit,

amounted to £16.13.4 per month, from which was deducted 3/- per day for messing plus stoppages for replacement of miscellaneous minor articles of kit or equipment. This was the first money I had ever earned. At White River I neither received any payment or my board for the first year as I was ostensibly learning to be a citrus grower despite doing manual labour (not supervision) alongside the African labourers from sunrise to sunset! To me this amount represented real wealth as, while not encouraging extravagant living – by any means – it certainly proved sufficient for a young recruit, all else being found.

The main extravagance of myself and fellow recruits consisted of going to the 'Lounge' for dinner of a Saturday night and then diagonally across the road from there to the pictures at the Palace Theatre. The Lounge was situated in First Street where Woolworths now stands, and Hampson & Lockie, the blacksmiths and farriers, occupied a stand close by. The Lounge was then owned and managed by Mr & Mrs Robinson, Snr, who for years lived at the corner of King George Road and Cambridge Road, Avondale; and in those days the Lounge provided a super dinner for 5/-.

The sole means of transport, unless one happened to be the proud possessor of a bicycle – a luxury which few recruits could afford – consisted of the homely ricksha, a most comfortable means of travelling a short distance in days when time and speed were of little importance, and infinitely preferable to 'shank's pony'.

Of an evening, especially at weekends, a cavalcade of rickshas would be drawn up outside the Police Depot and, when loaded with two occupants, would, for a stated nominal sum, proceed to town by way of a well worn path stretching diagonally from North Avenue through clumps of Msasa trees to Union Avenue near the Anglican Cathedral. These rickshas did a roaring trade and played a most important role before the arrival of the motor car. Like many others I mourn their passing and gratefully remember the service their 'drivers', for lack of a better word, provided.

One of the outstanding recollections I have of the recruits' course was the 6/7 weeks 'Mounted Column' undertaken by all the recruits undergoing training that July.

The 'Column' – consisting of a senior officer, the Chief Riding Instructor (Sgt. Major Hampton) and several of our instructors including a farrier and the said recruits – proceeded on horseback to traverse the greater part of the route taken by the Pioneer Column. The Column was accompanied by two/three wagons drawn by mules containing the horses' rations (crushed mealies plus a certain quantity of bran), rations for the entire contingent, home comforts, and all our kitbags containing blankets and spare clothing. Sleeping under the stars on the bare ground – with two blankets and a ground sheet – in front of a big camp fire was, in so far as I was concerned, an entirely novel, unforgettable and thrilling experience. The two Troops of recruits taking part were divided into small sections from each of which a Cook for the week was chosen, whose main duty was to prepare a hot meal nightly over an open fire. This was not an enviable task but all happily survived. It calls to mind the old story of the Orderly Officer for the day who, on entering the soldiers' mess, asked if there were any complaints? The Cook somewhat surprisingly complained he had been called a 'bastard', only to be met with a shout from an old soldier at the back of the room, 'What I want to know is, who called the bastard a cook?'

It was bitterly cold at times, especially at night, but the lesson as how to make oneself comfortable in the veld was soon learnt and after a couple of nights everybody slept the sleep of the just, or, anyway, just slept!

The horses were tethered by their headstall rimpies to a long line of short pieces of rope attached together and stretched between rows of trees, within a very short distance of their riders. Each section took it in turns for relays of its members to be on guard duty during the night for short intervals at a time. The usual routine was to break camp at dawn, outspan for a short breakfast, outspan for lunch when the horses were hobbled and put out to graze, and make camp for the night at about 3.30/4.00 p.m. To keep horses in fine fettle they had not only to be allowed ample time to graze each day but the Column proceeded at a 'walk march' throughout save for an occasional trot for a short distance early in the morning. Frequently the riders dismounted and led their horses – not so good.

Sunday was usually a rest day – most welcome to horses and riders alike, the latter taking the opportunity to wash and dry his underclothes. I well remember the Column crossing the Lundi River which was flowing swiftly at the time, as also the unforgettable sight of the crossing of the wagons, the mules being superbly handled by the Coloured Cape drivers – several of whom had arrived with the Pioneer Column. When outspanned across the Lundi the troops had a much needed swim while an N.C.O. sat on the bank with a loaded rifle to ward off any crocodiles which might venture too close. There was little, if any, danger in those days of becoming infected with Bilharzia, particularly in a fast flowing river.

The experience gained on the Column as to how to take proper care of one's horse and last, but not least, oneself in the veld proved invaluable when out on patrol subsequently in the outlying country districts. However, the return to 'Harari' and its bright lights, such as they were, was by no means unwelcome to horse and rider alike. For the next few weeks both recruit squads were busily engaged in ceremonial mounted escort drill in preparation for the arrival of Southern Rhodesia's first Governor, His Excellency Sir John Chancellor, on 29 September, 1923.

This event, a most memorable one forming as it did one of the stepping stones in Rhodesian history in marking the end of the Chartered Company era and the commencement of Responsible Government, went off splendidly. The Governor's Mounted Escort, much to the relief of the Commandant of Depot (Capt. Bugler) and the Chief Riding Instructor, lived up to expectations. To me, along with my fellow recruits and friends, including Jack Pithey (who subsequently became a Magistrate, Secretary to the Department of Justice and later became President of the Rhodesian Senate) this was a red letter day as also the hallmark of our recruits course.

The Annual Police Sports Day, consisting of mounted and foot events, took place a few days later. I, thanks to my horse *Ginger*, a treasure beyond price in the mounted events as he stood still when being mounted or dismounted and paid no attention to the excitement and confusion around him, had a most successful day.

Talking of this Sports Day calls to mind an amusing episode concerning 'Jock' Douglas. One of the highlights of the foot events was the African bicycle race, a source of great amusement to many, in which the Askaris (the African Police, so called, from the neighbouring African Training Depot) took part together with the Camp domestic servants and other Depot incumbents. It so happened in one of these races that the R.S.M.'s cook was leading the field in the final straight, well ahead of the other competitors. On observing this, 'Jock' shouted out enthusiastically, 'My cook-boy is winning, my cook-boy is winning!' At this stage the winning cyclist could no longer refrain from showing off before such a large and appreciative audience and took both hands off the handlebars. Nemesis quickly descended upon him for distaining the warning that pride comes before a fall. The exuberant rider, who had the race in his pocket, lost his balance, the bicycle deviated just short of the winning post, with the resultant pile-up of the overtaking cyclists. This caused roars of delight among the spectators in which 'Jock' took a realistic part but his delight was short-lived when he suddenly registered his cook was riding his (Jock's) bicycle. Amid the uproar could be heard Jock's furious shout, 'My ruddy cook-boy, My God, my ruddy bicycle'. History, unfortunately, does not relate the aftermath but it is certain that the malefactor never borrowed his master's bicycle again without the latter's knowledge or consent.

The stories about 'Jock' are legion and, although the following anecdote relates to a tragic happening, as it turned out, it bears repeating. Several years later one of the recruits failed to put in an appearance on an early Saturday morning Stables parade taken by the R.S.M. Not wishing to make an issue of it 'Jock' told his room-mate to go and fetch him and be quick about it. The former returned a few minutes later to report he was unable to awaken him. The Orderly Corporal for the day was then sent to rouse the defaulter but with no better success – he reported that the recruit appeared to be in a coma – to which 'Jock' replied in his inimitable manner;

'Nonsense, he is either drunk or playing possum'. The Orderly Sergeant was then instructed to proceed to the recruit's barrack room to inform him that if he was not on parade immediately he would be put on report. The Orderly Sergeant returned after a slightly longer interval and solemnly informed the R.S.M. that the recruit appeared to be dead. This evoked the immediate terse reply, 'He can't be dead, this is a Saturday and there's a Police rugger match this afternoon'. The R.S.M. accompanied by the Orderly Sergeant proceeded to the recruit's room where, after a cursory examination 'Jock' is reputed to have taken off his hat in respect and, sitting down on the spare bed, said, 'My God, he is dead. For heaven's sake somebody give me a "Flag" cigarette.' In telling this I do not wish the reader to form the wrong impression that 'Jock' was a somewhat callous person – he was in fact the kindest of humans and nobody was more genuinely and deeply distressed by this tragic occurrence than 'Jock' himself, now long gone to his well deserved rest.

Shortly after the Annual Sports day we recruits had our 'Passing Out' Parade which we all celebrated that evening in the Canteen, along with our Instructors, in the time honoured fashion and a very pleasant evening was had by all.

Our recruits course was over and the following day we dispersed and proceeded on transfer to our respective Districts and Outstations.

CHAPTER TWO
On Transfer to District Police

On leaving Depot I was transferred to Beatrice accompanied by my beloved chestnut horse *Ginger*, at my special request. This horse suited me from every point of view, being easy to handle, possessed of great courage and would not stray. He allowed his rider to fire off his back without becoming restive and, although horses are usually terrified of fire, permitted me on one occasion, when on patrol, to ride through a grass fire while expressing his natural fear and displeasure by snorting loudly. He would not shy at unexpected obstacles and had a most affectionate nature. One of his favourite habits was to nibble the back of my neck when being groomed and, when watered at the trough, would lift my stable hat from off my head and place it gently, crown uppermost, in the water.

After crossing the Hunyani drift (there were no low level or other road bridges in Rhodesia in 1923) the road to Beatrice can best be described as a sandy track intersected by about half a dozen wire fences with gates which I later became adept at opening without having to dismount even when leading another horse and pack mule (on my brief trips to Depot to have the horses shod).

The Beatrice Police Camp at that time was situated on the far side of the Umfuli River drift which latter, for several years, contained crocodiles in the deep pool immediately below the drift despite their being destroyed from time to time and shot at continuously.

The European Quarters mainly consisted of thatched pole and dagga rondavels with earthen floors hardened by many applications of dung and polished to a linoleum-like consistency. The stables were likewise somewhat primitive with a corrugated iron roof but provided an adequate and waterproof home for the three horses and two pack mules.

The Station Complement consisted of three European members, a Corporal (C.W.S. Twort) and two troopers including myself. I shared a rondavel with Trooper A. Carroll, invariably known as 'Bert'. Both Corporal Twort and Bert were seasoned campaigners, bedecked with medals, having served throughout the First World War, and were very experienced and capable policemen – needless to say, many years older than myself. There was an African N.C.O. and numerous Askaris (African Police Constables, also called the Black Watch). The hub of the Station was the 'Charge and Enquiry Office' which also served as a place in which Periodical Court was held once a month and presided over by a visiting Magistrate from Salisbury, although in those days Beatrice fell within the Hartley Police District with its headquarters at Hartley.

Cpl. Twort was a strict disciplinarian and a perfectionist but I am very grateful to both him and Bert Carroll for all they taught me about Police work in general and investigation of cases in particular. So much so that at the end of nine months when the names of would-be candidates for the next promotion exam for all ranks was called for, I, thinking it would be valuable experience for future examinations, had the temerity to submit my name. Much to my surprise, my application was recommended by Cpl. Twort and the District Police Superintendent which resulted in my being accepted as a Candidate by the Promotion Board, but more of this anon.

The first golden rule of police work which I learnt was to differentiate between inferences and facts and to prove the facts.

During those nine months while on mounted patrol I covered 1800 miles at an average of 200 per month. Horse sickness was still prevalent throughout most of Southern Rhodesia and the horses – the sole means of police transportation for patrol work in those days – had to be treated with all possible care, their temperatures being taken night and morning, 'per anum', without fail and if there was any rise in temperature had to be rested, whether on patrol or otherwise, until the temperature returned to normal. All patrols had to be carried out at a steady walk march (approx. 4 mph).

Mention of taking temperatures 'per anum' calls to mind the following allegedly true story. A young advocate appearing in Court for the first time was instructed to apply for judgement on a summons claim in the sum of X pounds together with interest at seven and a half per cent per annum and costs. Somewhat overcome by the occasion he nervously stammered out his application but when applying for interest he did so at the amount 'per anum', which evoked the immediate gentle response from the Judge, while maintaining an expressionless face but with a twinkle in his eye, 'Mr So-and-so, I have heard of persons paying through the nose before ...!'

Strict instructions were laid down in Standing Orders with regard to precautions to be taken against malaria and Blackwater fever which were very prevalent during the rainy season – mosquito nets had to be used and 5 grains of Government issue quinine taken every evening during the period 1st October to 30th April. These tablets were extremely bitter and were taken with the inevitable sun-downer.

In the event of Blackwater fever laying a policeman low while on patrol the great secret was not to move him. A coffin shaped hole was dug in the ground into which the patient was placed naked and covered with wet mud while he drank copious draughts of ordinary kaffir beer. He would be protected by the small patrol tent erected over him or, failing that, by a bivouac made of branches. He would remain there undergoing such treatment until his kidneys were functioning properly again and the fever literally sweated out of him, which treatment would normally take effect after three or four days. Many policemen have to thank this primitive method for saving their lives – the essence of the treatment being the immobilisation of the patient immediately the disease becomes apparent, combined with the sweating out treatment.

My customary monthly patrol was carried out in two parts – the European farming area north of the Umfuli River to the Hunyani River drift, 12 miles from Salisbury, and along the old Charter Road which branches off the Salisbury-Beatrice main road adjacent to where the Salisbury South Club now stands. The other part was through the Ganga Native Reserve on the far side of the Umfuli River, but this area was not patrolled so regularly during the rainy season. Each patrol lasted approximately a week and, where circumstances permitted, each European homestead was visited once a month.

In the European area the visiting trooper received a right royal welcome and most kindly hospitality and, when arriving in the late afternoon, was usually expected to stay the night. Obviously there were a few exceptions but one soon got to know where one was expected to stay the night as a matter of course and planned one's itinerary accordingly. I remember the kind hospitality shewn me by the following families – the Lintons of Carnoch, the Christians of Gilston, the Hughes, who farmed along the old Charter Road and the Hodsons of Gowerlands – among several others.

(Note: The Hodsons were the parents of Manfred Hodson, K.C. after whom the Manfred Hodson Hall at the University of Rhodesia is named. In the days of which I speak Manfred was a student at one of the South African Universities).

On the Native Reserve patrol, one visited all the main kraals and camped in the vicinity of such kraals close to running water, but not too close, on a rise in the ground if available and in the shade of Msasa trees. Firewood and cut grass for one's bed were invariably forthcoming and such delicacies as eggs, green mealies, sweet potatoes and the inevitable 'huku' (chicken) would be readily procurable for a few pence, if not a gift of welcome from the kraal head. A reasonably well-covered 'huku' would cost sixpence to one shilling, or a handful of salt by way of barter. Those were the days!

All drinking water was well boiled. The main beverages carried on patrol consisted of tea, Camp coffee and tins of sweetened condensed milk. Quaker oats, bread, rice and bacon together with the odd tin of sardines or bully beef, were the main standby.

On these patrols one was always accompanied by one or more Askaris, one's personal servant who attended to the cooking, under supervision, and carried the hurricane lantern, and faithful pack mule which carried the horse's rations and all other necessaries including my valise. To this day I still possess the same thick canvas valise, then complete with a roll-up cork mattress, that a dearly beloved aunt purchased for me at the Army and Navy Stores in London in 1923. It had my initials, name and B.S.A.P. emblazoned on it, complete with two broad leather straps with metal rings for attaching to the pack saddle. The valise was the perfect gift and I do not know what I would have done without it on patrol and on many subsequent camping out expeditions over the years. This valise, placed on top of a ground sheet resting on a thick bundle of cut veld grass, made the most wonderful bed imaginable, with one's saddle at the head of it forming a bed board. Many never to be forgotten nights under the glorious stars or perchance an African moon were spent on it, with my feet towards a large camp fire and *Ginger* tied to a tree close by but in such a manner that he could lie down on his bed of cut grass, if he so wished, and the pack mule alongside. The Africans, including prisoners and witnesses, would sleep on the opposite side of the fire which would be kept blazing throughout the night. They would also assist with the customary camp chores.

The population of Southern Rhodesia at this time was approximately 33,000 Europeans and 700,000 Africans, and to many of the latter, living in the Native Reserves, the only glimpse they got of a European was when a trooper was on patrol or when an Officer of the Native Department was collecting hut tax.

On arrival at a kraal all its occupants, men, women and children used to turn out and welcome us and after greetings had been exchanged and sundry police duties completed they invariably clustered around me seeking attention to their cuts, sores and sundry other ailments. I always carried with me on patrol an assortment of simple remedies with which I was able to administer first aid.

In those days Officials of the Native Department and Members of the Police were always treated with the greatest respect and awe especially by the rural Africans who invariably doffed their headgear, if any, when passing or meeting them and would unfailingly address them as 'Mambo' or 'Inkos'.

One of the many duties of members of the Police was to keep a register of all European residents in their area and keep up to date a map showing all roads, homesteads, stores and similar features. New homesteads, 'out in the blue', were frequently difficult to locate. I will never forget an occasion when, having to send the Native Constable ahead of me to visit certain native kraals on the edge of a reserve adjoining the European farming area while I made a detour to visit certain European farmers, a rendezvous was made for the night camping place at one of these new homesteads. Having completed the detour I made a bee line across the veld in the direction where the new homestead was supposed to be but without success. Fortunately, at about 4.30 p.m. I came across a few cows grazing apparently at random – this was a most welcome sight and happily anticipating someone would round up the cows before sunset I off-saddled to await developments. Sure enough within half-an-hour a herd boy turned up and directed me to the homestead – believe it or not, a bare quarter of a mile distant though completely concealed in a mass of thick bush, where I happily found the N.C. awaiting me and camp prepared for the night. Had it not been for those few cows I might quite easily have wandered for several miles, eventually having to spend the night in the veld without food or bedding, a most dismal prospect forsooth if not for anything else!

The risk of getting temporarily lost in the veld is always prevalent but, if the worst comes to the worst, a horse, if given his head and a loose rein, will usually find his way back safely to his stables.

In 1924, owing to an outbreak of East Coast fever in that area, no movement of cattle was allowed without the prior issue of a permit setting out full particulars including number of cattle, sex, colour, brands, markings, destination and the route to be followed – the latter being strictly enforced.

There was a large number of farmers of Afrikaner stock resident in the Beatrice, Featherstone and Enkeldoorn areas at that time, who used to proceed to Salisbury and back along the old Charter Road with their ox wagons and spans of oxen. One of their favourite devices was to sell some of the span in Salisbury or en route and return with replacements. One of my special duties was to patrol this road and examine all permits and check that the cattle corresponded to those stated therein. In many instances they didn't and the offending permit owner was duly summonsed to appear at the Beatrice Periodical Court, usually presided over by Mr T.C. Fynn, a well-known and highly esteemed Salisbury Magistrate. The accused always denied the charge and invariably accused me of making a mistake or giving false evidence. It was usually a question of the accused's word against mine. However, the presiding Magistrate accepted my sworn evidence in preference to that of the accused without exception – such evidence being supported by the production of my police note book containing the fullest particulars made at the time. This type of offence was very common at that period and, unfortunately, led to considerable ill-feeling against the police by the offenders.

In or about July, 1924, I proceeded to Salisbury to sit the promotion examination from Trooper to Corporal, never dreaming for one moment that I had the slightest chance of success. It proved quite an ordeal as, apart from many written papers, each candidate had to drill a squad of all the other candidates – consisting of Corporals, Sergeants and Sergeant-Majors – in front of the entire promotion board, headed by the Commissioner of Police, Col. Essex Capell, C.B.E., D.S.O. Having only left Depot about 10 months ago I was probably in a better position than many in so far as drill was concerned and, having nothing to lose, shouted out the commands at the top of my voice with gay abandon. If the former were not carried out to my satisfaction I repeated the same until the drill formation was, in my opinion, properly executed. I learnt later through the grapevine that this display on my part suitably impressed the promotion board as to my potential qualities of leadership and command. Being by far and away the youngest, I was only 21 at the time and the most inexperienced of all the promotion candidates, caused quite a sensation at my temerity in appearing, which was largely treated as a joke by my fellow candidates who, however, showed me considerable indulgence, kindness and comradeship.

The examination lasted several days and on its completion all candidates returned to their various Districts and Outstations.

Shortly after my return to Beatrice I proceeded on *Ginger* via the Ganga and Mandoro (*sic*) Natives Reserves to Hartley to take part in the annual shooting course which was held in relays – without any presentiment that I was leaving Beatrice for good. The next time I visited it, many years later, it would be as defending Attorney at the new Police Camp and Courthouse on the near side of the Umfuli River and, furthermore, all that would be left of the old police camp would be two lines of rather scraggy mulberry trees which used to grace the entrance to the camp.

Strange to relate, shortly before my retirement in March, 1971, I was asked by the Beatrice Women's Institute to give them a talk on legal matters affecting women's legal rights and disabilities, which, with the approval of the Law Society, I was delighted to do. It seemed passing strange but somehow befitting that my legal career should, in a manner of speaking, start and finish in the same place after an intervening period approaching fifty years.

While at Hartley I met for the first time other police members of the Hartley District including, among many others; Sgt. Appleby, later to become Commissioner of Police; Cpl. Verrall

who subsequently became Deputy Commissioner of the
Northern Rhodesian Police, thereafter Commissioner of Police
in the Bahamas; Staff Cpl. Jack Seaward who later became a
District Commissioner in the Colonial Service and Tpr. 'Curly'
Yeoman who, after retiring as Chief Inspector, years later
earned the distinction of then being the longest serving member
in the Police Reserve, from which he finally retired with the
rank of Captain.

At the end of the course I was taken to the Gatooma Hospital
and subsequently to the Salisbury General Hospital where I
was operated on for appendicitis by the then Mr Godfrey
Huggins, F.R.C.S. (later to become Sir Godfrey Huggins and
Prime Minister of Southern Rhodesia, for many years to hold
the record of being the longest serving P.M. in the British
Commonwealth. He eventually became Lord Malvern – the
name chosen being that of his old school – and P.M. of the
ill-fated Federation of Rhodesia and Nyasaland in which he was
succeeded by my old friend, Sir Roy Welensky).

While in hospital the promotion results appeared in Standing
Orders. To my utter amazement, not to say dismay, I was first
informed by my friend Patrick George Cookson, who had
recently joined the B.S.A. Police from England and was also in
hospital at that time, that my name was among the list of
successful candidates promoted from Trooper to Corporal. The
shock was somewhat lessened by the vain satisfaction in
knowing that I was the youngest Corporal ever to be promoted
in the B.S.A.P., at the age of 21. Admittedly I turned 22 within
a few weeks. The other consoling thought was a considerable
rise in pay. My promotion caused quite a lot of unfavourable
comment, needless to say, coupled with such remarks as:- Fancy
promoting that young squirt, he is still wet behind the ears!
What experience has he had of police work or running a Station?
– the truthful answer to such latter being none. Be that as it
may, the die was cast and I had no alternative than to face the
world with a smile, a somewhat wry one, but I derived considerable comfort from reminding myself of my life maxim – 'that
it is not the world that matters but the courage you bring to it'.

Reverting to Patrick George Cookson, he later became a life-
long friend as also godfather to one of my children –
affectionately known to them and my family as Patrick George
'Ruddy'. Subsequently he became a most gifted artist, not only
in painting horses and dogs for whom he had a particular

affinity, but also in writing poems which he also illustrated with delightful sketches, several of which have been published in publications overseas such as the *Field*.

While in hospital I was, as a great favour, allowed to watch Mr Huggins perform a three and a half hour operation on a male patient. Suitably masked and gowned I stood near the Anaesthetist, fascinated by this novel experience.

On leaving hospital I was immediately transferred to District Headquarters at Fort Victoria where I took over the duties of N.C.O. i/c the District Camp and Charge and Inquiry Office, but was not allowed to ride a horse for at least six months. The saddest thing about this promotion was my never seeing *Ginger* again – without even bidding him farewell – as, tragic to relate, *Ginger*'s days were numbered and during the ensuing wet season he succumbed to horse sickness. If ever a gallant steed deserved to graze in the 'Elysium Fields' *Ginger* did and never did a rider have a more courageous and splendid companion. I remember him with great affection to this day and often wonder whether had I remained at Beatrice I might have helped pull him through, but probably this is sentimental wishful thinking on my part.

I found the Fort Victoria District Police Camp a hard furrow to hoe, but under the kind guidance of Inspector Hewlett and the District Superintendent of Police (Capt. Hamilton), always known as 'Mickey', whose favourite expression when anything went amiss was 'It is arful, it is arful,' spoken with a broad Irish brogue, I learnt a lot about handling men and, on occasion, irate members of the public. I also gratefully remember the courtesy and kindness shown me by the Magistrate, Mr Deane-Simmons, when giving evidence in Court. This was particularly welcome as the Prosecutor, a Sergeant in the Town Police and one of the old hands, was by no means forthcoming or helpful, being inclined to let this young and ignorant N.C.O. stew in his own juice, in a manner of speaking! In years to come, when Mr Deane-Simmons was Chief Magistrate in Salisbury, I appeared before him as defending attorney on many occasions, only to receive the same kindness and courtesy as formerly.

On one never to be forgotten occasion, compliments from the Bench being an extremely 'rara avis', the same Magistrate congratulated me in my handling of a difficult case which he said should serve as a model. I mention this in all humility as the real credit lies with Providence who came to my timely assistance.

Mention of 'rara avis' calls to mind the following anecdote concerning a dear old lady whose main delight was in attending civic functions in the City of London. On one such occasion she found herself seated at luncheon between an eminent K.C. and a well-known surgeon. During a lull in the conversation she turned to the learned Counsel saying, 'Oh, Mr So-and-so, I have been following your latest case with great interest and note that the words "Virgo intacta" frequently appeared, what exactly do they mean?' Counsel, momentarily taken aback by this indelicate question, suggested that it would be a more suitable question to be answered by his medical friend on her right. On referring the question to the surgeon he, on noticing Counsel's almost imperceptible wink, asked her if she had heard the expression 'rara avis' before? 'Oh yes', said the dear old lady, 'and I know what it means.' 'Well,' replied the surgeon, 'a virgo intacta is exactly the same thing, only slightly rarer!'

Col. Carbutt was the Provincial Commissioner and his good lady, possessed of considerable musical talent, used to regale the worthy local citizens with pleasant musical evenings, supported by a small orchestra in which, in a weak moment, I was inveigled to play the swanee whistle with, it is regretted, very limited success.

Other well-known characters in that area were Dr Jim Kennedy of Ndanga, beloved by all and sundry; Sgt. Keogh of Gutu who had the deserved reputation of being one of the best linguists and prosecutors in the police; the ranchers Messrs. Sommerville and Dot; and in particular Tom Murray McDoughall of 'Triangle' fame who first introduced sugar to the Lowveld and subsequently had a lake named in his honour. Mention must also be made of a notorious character known as 'French Marie' of whom not only her African employees stood in awe but also some members of the Police. She dressed like a man in breeches and long riding boots, had short hair, spoke like a man and her language on occasions was a real treat. She always carried a sjambok with which, so rumour had it, she meted out rough and ready justice to her employees who learnt to obey her implicitly and held her in great esteem if not affection. Be all that as it may, beneath this rugged exterior beat a very kindly heart, if not one of pure gold. Tales of her exploits are numberless.

I humbly remember an amusing 'bona fide' misunderstanding

between Inspector Hewlett, myself and a friend of mine, Staff Cpl Maslin, in which both Corporals were suitably corrected and pleasantly rebuked. The law uses certain Latin expressions which from time immemorial are pronounced in the most abominable Latin-cum-pidgin English, from a Latin scholar's point of view. One of these is when a case is postponed 'sine die' (without mention of any date to which it is postponed), pronounced 'signee die'. Neither of us had heard this expression in Court before and were nonplussed when Inspector Hewlett pronounced it in the way he did. Noting the surprised expression on our two faces he kindly explained it to us, ending up by saying, 'I would have thought both of you having had a classical education would know the meaning of these two simple Latin words, which evoked the immediate response, 'Oh, you mean "sinnay deeay" (pronounced as spelt) to which he justifiably replied, 'I pronounce it the way it is pronounced in the Courts – the correct way – and the sooner you two learn to pronounce it that way the better'.

He kindly accepted the forthcoming apologetic explanation to the reason for the misunderstanding being due to lamentable ignorance on the listeners' behalf and there the matter ended on a happy note, but I never forgot the lesson learnt on that occasion that things are not always what they appear at first sight or, for that matter, sound.

Talking about 'bona fide' misunderstandings calls to mind the rather nice little tale concerning a young naval cadet at Osborne attending an end of term dance. He noticed a young damsel in her late teens or early twenties sitting out at the beginning of a dance so – in true naval tradition – went up to her and asked if he might have the pleasure of this dance. The young lady was eyeing a naval lieutenant, unattached at the time, in no uncertain manner and on receiving this courteous request looked the young cadet up and down in a cold and haughty manner before replying ungraciously, 'I am not in the habit of dancing with children', which evoked the immediate courteous response, 'Madam, please accept my most humble apologies – I stupidly did not notice your condition'.

One good thing accomplished by my promotion indirectly resulted in Trooper Richens becoming a Commissioned Officer – 'Richie', a bemedalled member of World War 1 vintage was an excellent police trooper of many years' standing and experience as also a first class linguist in the Shona language. One evening over sundowners he was ribbing me about my early promotion and seemed somewhat surprised when I replied it was no use ribbing me, why in heaven's name did he not do something about it himself as he could hardly expect to get promoted if he could not be bothered to send his name forward to sit the exam; and to get on with it. Richie obviously gave this suggestion favourable consideration as he applied to sit for the next examination which he passed with flying colours. From there he went from strength to strength and, within a short while, obtained his Commission. If my recollections are correct Richie retired with the rank of Major.

Having failed to recuperate as quickly as expected due to suspected adhesions, I returned to Salisbury General Hospital for treatment and observation. While in hospital I met Trooper 'Paddy' Pentland (later a member of the Native Department, now alas many years deceased) who became my life-long friend. Paddy was the proud possessor of a lovable white bull terrier bitch called Bessie, a universal favourite among the European members of the Force but a menace to the Africans by whom she was treated with great caution. Her end was as sudden and unexpected as it was tragic and unique. Paddy was then stationed at Mtoko and Bessie, as always, slept under his bed. It was Paddy's custom to leave his door open at night. One moonlight night he was awakened by a scream from Bessie and a commotion under his bed. He leapt out of bed, grabbed his loaded sporting rifle, rushed to the door just in time to see a large leopard carrying off Bessie across the open square. Releasing the safety catch he fired one round at the leopard, dropping it dead in its tracks, but, alas, he was too late to save Bessie whose neck was broken. For sheer audacity on behalf of the leopard this takes some beating, and although hard to believe is a perfectly true story, which bears out the saying, 'truth is stranger than fiction'.

After a short stay in hospital I was transferred to Wedza as N.C.O. i/c, my first command of an Outstation – but before narrating my experiences at such Outstation, I wish to mention two noteworthy performances, among many others, by past members of the B.S.A.P.

The first relates to the longest ever serving member who retired in 1943, having joined the Force in 1907 – Inspector W. Hughes-Hall, M.S.M., M.B.E. (Regimental No. 939) and on retiring became a temporary staff member of the Public Health

Department where he carried out his duties 'inter alia' as the Workmens Compensation Representative at the North Avenue African Hospital until 1958, thereby completing 50 years and 252 days service with the S.R. Government. H.H., as he is invariably known, was awarded the Pioneer Golden Axe for his services to the Pioneers, Early Settlers and B.S.A. Co. Police as also their Majesties' Silver Jubilee medal in 1935 for his long and loyal service to the B.S.A.P. He has been a member of the Police Regimental Association since 1926 and is probably the earliest historian of the Force, having collected 200 photos of distinguished ex-members of the B.S.A.P., together with medals, including a V.C. and swords, which collection is preserved in the Police (Morris) Depot Sergeants Mess in Salisbury. During my time in the Police H.H. acted 'in loco parentis' to the recruits in Depot, putting them wise as regards all their duties while regaling them with countless accounts of the Force since its inception and imbuing them with its famous traditions.

The other relates to an old friend of mine – Andrew Pickup – now living at Minnehaha in the Inyanga District, one of the finest amateur middle-weight boxers I have ever seen, who had the distinction of winning the S.R. middle and heavy-weight amateur championships about 1922. He also entered and won the heavy-weight Police Championships in 1923, thus leaving 'Smiler' Auret, another outstanding Police boxer, to win the middle-weight championship in 1924. Andrew competed in the S.A. Olympic Trials as a middle-weight when he was just beaten on points in the semi-finals by McCorkindale, brother of the famous professional, Don McCorkindale.

CHAPTER THREE
Wedza

Wedza, regarded by many Force members as being one of the favourite and healthiest Outstations in Rhodesia, is situated approximately midway between Marandellas and Buhera (Charter District), to the south of Marandellas. The Wedza and Buhera Districts are divided by the Sabi River which flows at the foot of majestic Mount Wedza.

Wedza itself in those days merely consisted of the Native Department with an Assistant Native Commissioner, then Assistant Magistrate, and usual complement of African Native officials, and the Police Camp consisting of the N.C.O. i/c, one Trooper, African Constables and two African Lock-up Warders. Apart from the Wedza and Soswe Reserves the district was a prosperous European farming area producing excellent tobacco and beef cattle.

It was here that my legal career really got going in earnest as one of my main duties was prosecuting in the local Court, which, depending on circumstances, frequently sat several times a week. Prosecuting also involved the framing of indictments, preparing all cases for trial including the interrogation of witnesses, taking of statements and issuing process. I soon learned to type efficiently – a four fingered exercise using two fingers of each hand.

In addition to normal Police duties including keeping the Occurrence Book (the Policeman's Bible in which every occurrence is meticulously entered) right up-to-date in chronological order, rendering endless returns and reports to District H.Q., and drilling and inspecting the Native Police. I was also Lock-up Keeper and Issuer of sundry permits in respect of which, including prosecuting, I received extra pay which enabled me to save almost my entire salary. Messing was maintained at 3/- a day and for that sum one could live remarkably well as the N.C.O. i/c kept a few sheep, hens and chickens including the odd cow or two, which on his transfer were paid for and taken over for a nominal sum by his successor. Vegetables in ample supply were home grown. The stock and vegetable garden were looked after by short term prisoners or occasionally by detainees awaiting summary trial for minor offences.

The majority of the European farmers could be visited by daily patrols, most of the latter being carried out by Trooper Grimmet, an experienced policeman who, prior to his transfer to Wedza was stationed at Mount Darwin. He was the Chief Investigating Officer in the famous Darwin 'Rain Goddess' case which aroused great general interest and was reported at length in several columns of the *London Times*. Trooper Grimmet was of invaluable assistance to me throughout my sojourn at Wedza.

My predecessor i/c of Police Wedza was Cpl. Sawyer, subsequently to become head of one of the departments in the Shell Company in Capetown and the father, a few years later, of Sydney who later became Parliamentary Secretary (Deputy

Minister being its equivalent today) to Sir Malcolm Barrow, then Minister of Defence, Economic Affairs and Power in the Federal Government of Rhodesia and Nyasaland. By strange coincidence Sydney became articled to me at the age of 17 – later becoming a partner and remained with me for the next twenty years or so. Sydney, who had a decided 'yen' for politics, became an M.P. at 27 and, when made Federal P.S. to Sir Malcolm Barrow in May, 1962 at the age of 31, was the youngest appointed Minister in Rhodesian history.

Richard Wolton, afterwards Managing Director of Fisons for the Rhodesias and Nyasaland, was appointed Cattle Inspector for the Wedza District and lived and messed in the Police Camp (where he kept his buggy and two mules), thus forming a very happy trio. Richard was a delightful character and a friendship sprang up between him and me which, despite our paths crossing only rarely since those days, still endures. The writer well remembers an occasion when the late John Kerr (subsequently Chief Native Commissioner) then a junior Assistant in the Native Department stationed at Buhera, arrived at the Police Camp just in time to partake of a hearty and well-deserved breakfast, having cycled from Buhera across the Sabi River en route to Marandellas where he was to continue his journey by train to Salisbury – to play in a rugby match. He was a renowned rugby player but rumour had it that he was then courting a girl in Salisbury, whom he eventually married, so was able to kill two birds with one stone but, be that as it may, his performance in cycling that distance was a remarkable feat by any standard. My time was fully occupied in the 'C & I' office, but I did manage to visit most, if not all, the European farmers in my area from time to time. I also once managed to complete the Wedza Reserve Patrol to the junction of the Sabi and Macheke rivers, a lovely wild piece of country, which was the furthest boundary of the Wedza Police area.

The period spent at Wedza was beyond question the happiest of my five years in the Police. The farming community was a truly delightful one and to this day I gratefully remember the kindness and hospitality invariably shown me as also many of their names including their farms. Among others; The Darrolls at 'Shaka'; the Seagers at 'Nelson'; the famous and well-beloved sportsman John Hopley at 'Fair Adventure', his wife and family; the Skorrors (who took over the former B.S.A. Co. settlement near the Postal Agency at Inoro, adjacent to the Ruzawi River) and their assistants Frank Scott and Andy Young; Monty Laurie, a renowned personality and his friend and assistant Levett, who farmed near Inoro; Major Fleming and his wife and family at 'Collace'; the Spicers at 'Chiswana'; the Dryboroughs at 'Mari'; the Rutherfords at 'Igava' and the Nuttal-Smiths near Shaka.

(*Note*: *In 1974 Major Fleming later returned to Rhodesia for the opening of the new 'Fleming Hospital' in Salisbury, named after his father, the late Col. Fleming, the famous pioneer doctor who for many years was Medical Director and was the Chief B.S.A.P. Medical Superintendent for very many years*).

Tennis was then the main pastime and tennis parties were held regularly at weekends. I used to ride over on horseback to either the Darrolls, the Seagers or the Skorrors, their farms being within a reasonable distance of the Police Camp, play tennis all afternoon or occasionally all day on a Sunday, and then ride back in the evening.

Police inspections were from time to time carried out by the D.S.P. from Salisbury who travelled in a buckboard drawn by mules. His arrival in the Wedza area was always heralded by a telephone call from a neighbouring farmer saying 'old so-and-so has just passed through heading in your direction', which timely warning enabled me to make sure that everything was more or less ship-shape before the Inspecting Officer put in an appearance. One of the items beloved of Inspecting Officers was to satisfy himself that the chest containing the medical supplies (always known as medical comforts and invariably kept under lock and key), contained its full complement and, in particular, that the brandy bottle contained its proper quantity of brandy. There have been occasions when this precious bottle has been known to contain anything but brandy. On many occasions when the private supply of this delectable liquor suddenly ran out, 'dop and ginger' being a universal favourite among members of the Force for the inevitable sundowner, this called for a little surreptitious borrowing from the 'Medical Comforts' and its consequent replenishment, which at times was overlooked. However, a quick telephone call to a neigh-bouring farmer, followed by the instant dispatch of a Native Constable on his bicycle, would inevitably rectify that inadver-tent sin of omission and timeously at that. In those days every district Native Police member possessed a bicycle for which he was paid an official allowance.

Two cases stand out foremost in my memory. The one concerned an alien native, employed at the Wedza Mine, who appeared before the A.N.C. on a preparatory examination on a charge of raping an African woman. The accused was unable to speak or understand the Shona language, in which the A.N.C. was an adept, or for that matter any other language known to the African Court interpreter. In sheer desperation as a last resort I, in my capacity as Public Prosecutor, suggested that the interpreter should try Cha-lapa-lapa (kitchen kaffir). The writer will never forget the disgust and anger displayed by the A.N.C., a somewhat touchy individual at the best of times, whose 'amour propre' could, alas, be so easily injured. The A.N.C. glared at me in such a manner I feared I might be held in contempt of Court at any moment. It was, however, a matter of 'Hobsons Choice', as it was the only language the wretched accused understood. However, after a lengthy discussion between the Court and myself, as Public Prosecutor, which I conducted with the utmost tact I could muster, the Court reluctantly agreed to this obnoxious procedure being followed and the accused was duly committed for trial on the charge of rape. The accused was duly indicted for the High Court in Salisbury and, to my satisfaction in so far as the language question was concerned, he was convicted of that charge.

Talking about rape reminds me of the following anecdote:- An accused charged with that far too common crime was defended by learned Counsel. The learned Judge was not too favourably impressed by the submissions made by Counsel to the Complainant in cross-examination in an endeavour to prove that she was a consenting party by reason of her feeble resistance, tantamount to apathetic acquiescence on her part. He kept on interrupting him saying, 'Mr So-and-so, surely if the complainant was in fact consenting she would have behaved in such-and-such a fashion, or not acted in such-and such a way.' Counsel, somewhat exasperated by these interruptions from the Bench, having hitched up his gown, with dignity addressed the Court in these words: 'My Lord, with great respect, I bow to your Lordship's superior knowledge in the matter' – he then sat down.

The other case concerned a well-known and highly esteemed benign African Witchdoctor (a herbalist/*nganga* as opposed to the evil type of witchdoctor, a *maroyi*) called Chivangu, who lived in the Buhera District and had committed the heinous crime of theft by false pretences in that he threw the bones for an African client, told him his fortune and demanded and was paid a reasonable fee for such services. Had he not charged for his services he would have committed no offence at law. His European counterpart when telling fortunes goes about it in a more discreet way by making no charge – merely leaving it to the discretion and generosity of the customer to put a little crisp something in the attractive bowl ostentatiously displayed on a table nearby – which the customer invariably does. The difference in law between these two approaches seems somewhat puzzling and illogical to both lawyer and layman alike.

Be that as it may, Chivangu, having committed the offence within the Wedza Magisterial area, was arrested and brought to Camp. I received a deputation from the African Corporal and several African Constables with the unusual request that the accused should not be locked up pending trial but should be allowed to live in the African Police lines where they would look after him and be responsible for his safe custody. After interviewing the accused, a most respectful and courteous old African, and obtaining his parole I accepted the responsibility of granting their request. The accused's delight and gratitude expressed by the clapping of his hands and an effusion of thanks, was ample reward for the slight risk involved. On appearing in Court he was duly convicted and sentenced to pay a fine of £5 which was paid then and there. Before leaving the Camp he willingly threw the bones for me – but without any reward on this auspicious occasion – foretelling many things concerning my future which, believe it or not, came to pass as predicted.

Chivangu was a seer like the soothsayers of old and I never heard of him using his talents for destructive purposes. Thereafter, if ever I required vital police information the same was forthcoming, in confidence, if it lay within Chivangu's power to supply it. This usually was the case and so, in this instance, the relaxation of customary legal procedures paid off handsomely to the benefit of good police relations and justice as a whole.

Early in 1926, a Census of the European population was carried out. This involved all the European members of the Police Force in the country districts, duly appointed Census Officers, having to deliver, explain and ensure that the forms were properly filled in and to subsequently collect the same. This was a considerable task 'per se' with the result that ordinary police duties and Court work had to take second place, with the consequent backlog of cases steadily increasing, much to the annoyance of the aforesaid A.N.C. who put in an unfavourable report to the Authorities concerning me. Fortunately for me the Director of Census, Mr Nanson, submitted a contradictory report, stating 'inter alia' that I had carried out my Census duties, in most difficult circumstances, to his entire satisfaction, so no more was heard of the matter. Prior to my departure the said A.N.C. was transferred and replaced by a very pleasant person who happened to be a keen tennis player and we got on like a house on fire.

While at Wedza I completed my initial three years' service and was now entitled to take six months leave on full pay conditional on signing on for a further two years. Although proceeding on long leave invariably meant losing one's station I deemed it advisable – having saved a considerable amount of money meanwhile – to take it without delay, the next period of long leave only falling due three years from the date of my return to duty.

Having said goodbye to many of my new-found friends I left Wedza with a sore heart. The French have a charming way of expressing what I felt, *'Partir c'est un peu mourir'*. I little dreamt that I would return there on several occasions many years hence to defend cases in the same Court in which I started prosecuting as also to bring out a tennis team from Salisbury – called 'Roger and his Lodgers' – to play a Wedza team at the Wedza Country Club – an annual event – and so meet again many of my old friends and play against some of their children who were now grown up with families of their own.

CHAPTER FOUR
Battlefields *et seq*

On return from long leave, happily spent with my parents and sister at their home in N. London near Kenwood and the Highgate Ponds, I, for my sins of commission or omission, was posted to Battlefields in the Hartley District with its District Headquarters now removed to Gatooma.

Battlefields, which lies alongside the line of rail somewhere half way between Gatooma and Que Que, is – with the exception of a portion of the Rhodesdale Estate – to all intents and purposes a mining area and exceedingly hot in more ways than one. A greater contrast to Wedza including scenery, climate and inhabitants can hardly be imagined. Generally speaking the Police at that time were by no means 'persona grata' among the mining fraternity and in many instances were regarded as interfering busy bodies. There were of course many worthy exceptions among whom, among others I gratefully remember in particular Mr and Mrs Alex Kerr of the Devon Mine.

While at Battlefields I was selected to represent my fellow Corporals in the Hartley District at the Annual Police Conference held in Salisbury. During my absence on long leave certain changes in the Police Contract and Conditions had taken place which were to form one of the main items placed on the Agenda and provoked a considerable amount of acrimonious feeling and discussion. Unwarily stepping in where angels fear to tread I unwisely proposed a resolution tantamount to a vote of no confidence in the Government for changing the police conditions of service to the detriment of the Force without the members being given the opportunity of expressing their views at the Annual Conference, or words to that same meaning and effect. The resolution, having been seconded and carried by a large majority of votes went forward to the then Police Commissioner, Col. Stops, C.B.E., for his consideration and comments.

At the conclusion of the Police Conference, which lasted several days, it was customary for the Commissioner to address the Conference and express his views on the various resolutions which, on this occasion, he did in no uncertain manner. In fact, from the moment he entered the Conference room it was obvious he was in no conciliatory mood – far from it. Looking as black as thunder straight at me, he started off by saying, somewhat unexpectedly but, beyond any reasonable doubt, ominously, 'I consider there are far too many Corporals in the Corps.' Having delivered this broadside he continued dealing with the resolution proposed by me which he considered a personal vote of no confidence in himself as Police Commissioner and at which he took the strongest exception. Whether he was right or wrong in so surmising it is not for me to say, but it was not intended to cast that reflection. Suffice it is to say, I was left in no doubt that I was 'persona non grata' in so far as the Commissioner was concerned at that precise moment.

The writing was on the wall and on my return to Battlefields, having an unhappy premonition of things to come, I set about putting the camp in spick and span condition. This meant whitewashing the stones leading up to and surrounding the camp, seeing that all rifles, saddlery, kit and equipment were spotlessly clean, including that of the African Police and ensuring that all police dockets, records, returns and such like were right up to date. Just as well I did for within a few weeks the Police Commissioner carried out a surprise inspection. Having completed a meticulous inspection he informed me that I was very good on paper but that the camp was filthy and disgusting, a terminological inexactitude if ever there was one, and even the chimney pots were crooked. I tactfully refrained from suggesting that the chimney pots hardly fell within my jurisdiction as N.C.O. i/c and in any event the same had been erected years ago by the Police Pioneer detachment (the name given to the building department of the B.S.A.P.).

However, taking it all in all, the Inspection went off far better than anticipated and the parting took place, if not exactly 'en rapport' with one another, on reasonable terms. Be that as it may, 'forewarned is forearmed', so expecting another inspection shortly by the District Superintendent, I did not let up in any way. My anticipation was soon justified. However on this occasion everything went according to plan, but the D.S.P. thinking he must make some unfavourable comment in all the circumstances, however slight, having noticed a clean tablecloth on the Mess table inspected it carefully and having done so was, with almost a sigh of relief, now in a position to enter one very minor adverse comment in the Occurrence Book, which he did in red ink in the following exact words:- 'I consider that a Mess tablecloth, if used, should be hemmed.'

The law has a trite saying, 'de miminis non curat lex' (the law does not concern itself over very trivial matters) so I was not unduly perturbed by this mildest of Pygmalion criticisms and although the said criticism, from which I derived considerable amusement ever since, will not be found written on my heart when I die the recollection will remain with me until I do.

The camp having been described as to its worst aspects – namely the chimney pots – the best was undoubtedly its tennis court on which I played many enjoyable singles against the two troopers – 'Selous' Hamilton, always called Selous because he was notoriously keen on shooting game, and Paddy Malone, a wild Irishman possessed of the broadest brogue and an irrepressible sense of humour. At the weekend social tennis used to be the order of the day, this being the sole form of recreation and entertainment available.

Not long after the above inspections I was transferred to Salisbury Depot, along with two or three Corporals from other districts, including A.S. Hickman (Hicky) and Frank Rowley (the former later became Commissioner of Police, the latter Assistant Commissioner), ostensibly for the purpose of being vetted for Police Commissions in the not too distant future.

While in the Depot I assisted the Chief Riding Instructor (S/Major Hampton) with the newest joined recruits and in training re-mounts which latter was great fun and most rewarding. Another, by no means pleasant, task allotted to me was to ride horses that had caused serious injury to riders on outstations and then write a report on them recommending their retention in the Force after additional training or their subsequent disposal by sale on the market square, without warranty. I have good reason to remember one particular large grey horse with a mouth like iron who had the unenviable reputation of suddenly bolting at full gallop for no apparent reason with his head up in the air as far as it would stretch. This 'star gazing', so called, prevented him from seeing where he was going and he would then stop absolutely dead with the inevitable result to the unfortunate rider; the last of whom, being so seriously injured, was obliged to leave the Force, this being the decision of his medical board.

On the day in question I was riding the grey in the direction of Gun Kopje when, for no apparent reason, the horse threw its head in the air, turned and suddenly bolted in the direction of the Avondale–Mazoe–Bindura railway line, which in those days meandered between the Police Depot and the Salisbury prison. A train happened to be approaching at the time but the horse beat it to the crossing and then made blindly across country for a clump of trees. By leaning right over the horse's neck I managed to catch hold of its bridle close to the bit and, using all my strength, managed to pull its head round which compelled the horse to move in a circle until eventually it was brought to a halt within a few feet of the trees and could be dismounted. Thanks to Providence I survived to tell the tale – needless to say my subsequent report resulted in the grey being sold on the Market square without warranty, but with the timely warning that this horse was dangerous, a bolter and 'star gazer'.

Shortly after this incident in 1928, I proceeded on another long column, similar to that experienced by me when a recruit, in company with fellow Corporals Hickman and Rowley. On this occasion the Column moved in the opposite direction towards the Fungwe Reserve and the Makaha Mine, north of the Mazoe River, far beyond Shamva. While in the Fungwe Reserve the African mine employees in the Shamva Mine went on strike and took possession of the Shamva Hill. Members of the Column were hastily recalled by use of lorries and driven straight to Shamva through the night, the horses meeting them later. Having disembarked, they cleared the Hill at dawn with fixed bayonets, driving the employees before them back to the Mine until they could be surrounded – thus averting a nasty situation. When things had calmed down the Column resumed its way along the Mazoe Valley.

Among the recruits taking part in the Column were Troopers John Lombard and Graham Rolfe (both later to become Assistant Commissioners of Police), Waddy and Rose. On return from the Column I wrote a satire about it in the form of conversations between the horses ridden by different ranks from the Officer Commanding the Column downwards, which caused a considerable amount of amusement and the raising of eyebrows in certain quarters when published in the Police Magazine, the *Outpost*. The writer claims no originality for the idea which was cribbed from Kipling's 'Mules' but, needless to relate, any further literary similarity abruptly ended there and then.

On completion of two further years of service and wishing to pursue my legal career in a more direct manner I applied for and obtained an appointment in the District Courts branch of the S. Rhodesian Civil Service.

So ended five exceedingly happy years spent in the B.S.A.P.; a wonderful experience for a youngster to learn about the Country and her indigenous inhabitants, to say nothing of the legal experience gained by me from the police angle which was to prove of the greatest benefit and assistance throughout the remainder of my legal career. I have also maintained the closest and friendliest association with the Force and its Regimental Association, of which latter I am not only a life member but, on the death of a then fellow Attorney, Major J.E. Nicholls, O.B.E. circa the beginning of World War 2, had the privilege of replacing him as Hon. Legal Adviser to the Association, until my retirement from active practice in 1971.

I wish to conclude this part of my memoirs by narrating the following true story which it is hoped may be appreciated particularly by those sportsmen who, on occasions, when out shooting guinea fowl on the veld and unable to get such running birds to fly have, in sheer desperation, fired at them willy nilly!

A young B.S.A. Policeman, having been stationed for several years at an Outstation, returned overseas on his first long leave. He decided to have a go at the partridges and his father, thinking he might be a little rusty, wisely decided that the Headkeeper should accompany him – but to little avail. While walking through the stubble they disturbed a covey of partridges which started to run.

To the Headkeeper's amazement and utter dismay his protégé raised his gun to his shoulder. In a voice of horror tinged with apprehension he cried out, 'Sir – surely you are not going to fire at a running bird.' The reply followed instantly – 'No ruddy fear, I am going to wait until it stops.'

LOMAGUNDI PATROL

Herbert Montagu Surgey
Captain (1860) British South Africa Police

Note: Published in The Outpost *in November 1967. Captain Surgey attached this comment to his article:*
~ In recent months, members of the Force who might have thought of the Lomagundi area as just another district of our vast country, have been given first-hand knowledge of the terrain and of the hardships to be experienced in the region. There is no truer axiom than that history repeats itself and thirty-eight years ago there was a parallel ignorance and more than a hint of a problem in the wild stretches of the Lomagundi Valley. I must apologise to readers for any inaccuracies or omissions in this rehashed patrol report, the original of which was submitted to the then Commissioner, Colonel George Stops, C.B.E., in 1929. In writing it now, I have had to rely on my memory and some photographs taken by a fellow member of the patrol, Trooper Jack Hoddinott.

In 1929, the Native Affairs Department in the Lomagundi District became disturbed at the increasing number of baptisms by total immersion of converts to the Watch Tower movement. As far as I can recollect, this movement was potentially subversive and aimed at an uprising against the white man after the arrival of a saviour – a mythical figure known as Rei Maria.

There was no evidence that this brand of Watch Tower movement was even remotely connected with the Watch Tower Bible and Tract Society. Its aims were totally different. One could have no quarrel with the concept of baptism but when the new man emerging from the water was dedicated to ultimate violence, the prospects, however remote, were disturbing to say the least.

The late Charles Bullock, the Native Commissioner at Sinoia, was well informed regarding the Watch Tower leaders and the areas in which the movement was gaining ground. These were north of Sinoia, between the Angwa and Hunyani Rivers up to the Zambesi Escarpment; west of Sinoia up as far as the Sanyati River; and in the remoter areas of the Urungwe Reserve with the northern extremity at the present-day road from Makuti to Lake Kariba.

Our information was that Watch Tower converts took comfort from the belief that, man for man, the African was inferior to his rival only because he lacked modern fire-arms and mechanical transport. In the following respects they felt that they could more than hold their own;

1. Their ability to move around the country without the aid of a guide.
2. Their ability to walk long distances, if necessary carrying a load.
3. Their lack of dependence upon camping equipment and the paraphernalia considered by the European essential for a trip into the interior.
4. Their ability to live off the country.
5. Their possession of a degree of toughness not normally found among white men who were more accustomed to soft living.

Such was the picture in the eyes of the members of the Watch Tower and it was decided at high level that the time had come for a reappraisal of the white man's alleged defects.

Arising from this decision, it was agreed that, as Officer Commanding the Lomagundi District, I was the obvious person to lead a strong patrol consisting of ten experienced veldmen and twenty police Askari (Government House Guards) into the Watch Tower areas for a period of approximately three weeks. Our method of transport was to be two six-wheeler Thorneycroft lorries, hired from the Transport Department and to be driven by George Schlacter (Junior) and Jimmy Powell.

Our duties were clear. We were to demonstrate to the best of our ability that we were capable of holding our own with the inhabitants of the area in the five points mentioned above. In American parlance, it was a 'tough assignment' but my hand-picked patrol fully accepted the challenge. As physical endurance was of paramount importance, members of the patrol were encouraged to provide themselves with thick crepe-soled boots in addition to the issue variety. Foot injuries were to be avoided at all costs. Fishing rods and shotguns could be carried on the lorries as, though this was to be no normal police patrol, we would have to live off the country and be in a position to trade meat for milk, eggs, pumpkins and so forth. Infantry pattern webbing equipment was issued to all so that when necessary, rolled blankets, ground sheets and valises could be carried by each man.

The patrol was divided into two sections of five Europeans and ten Askari, each section being allocated to one of the two lorries.

There were no servants. Each man attended to his own washing and general chores. For messing purposes, five men made up each mess. When on the move, supplies were distributed to each man in the section, one man carrying his mess flour and baking powder, another the bacon and eggs packed in mealie meal, another the tea, coffee, sugar and so on. Bread making was the responsibility of the two drivers, George Schlachter and Jimmy Powell who stayed with their lorries while the rest of us were absent on patrol and they made a splendid job of the baking.

After leaving Sinoia, it was decided that the first challenge would be to scale the approach to the Mount Tchetchenini massif by a direct route up and down parallel ridges of thickly bushed country. Mount Tchetchenini lies between the Angwa and Hunyani Rivers and was deep in the heart of Watch Tower country.

We arrived at some kraals approximately ten miles as the crow flies from the mountain and enquired from the local populace how long it would take us to reach our objective by the normal approach – paths in the shape of an elongated 'vee' which skirted the eastern edge of the ridges. We were told that the journey would take 'rather more than a day' and when informed of our proposed route, the Africans were emphatic that it was impossible to travel directly across the ridges as there were no paths. Sticking our necks out, we mentioned that we not only intended to reach the mountain but to return to the kraals the same day and that we required the services of two locals who could follow us and assist in transporting back to the camp any game meat which we might shoot. Our real purpose in finding local Africans to accompany us on the march was that we should have independent witnesses to the extent of our travels.

We left at dawn the next morning and shot for the pot as we made our way up and down the ridges mainly aided by compass bearings. With Mount Tchetchenini towering over us in the sunlight, we paused only for 'brunch' at noon, a meal of porridge, grilled guinea fowl and/or bush buck, potatoes, flap-jacks and coffee. We achieved our purpose and arrived back at the kraals late in the afternoon, footsore and weary but triumphant. The issue of a tot of Dop and copious swigs of kaffir beer (grand stuff for keeping the kidneys in order) soon made us forget our tiredness. Before we moved to our camping site near the Angwa River, we presented the locals with gifts of meat and in return, received a cheery send-off.

We had completed our first task satisfactorily and hoped that we had made the desired impression in regard to lesson number one as read with four and five, but at this stage there was no means of knowing.

The following morning we came across a kraal school in Chief Bepura's country. There was an African teacher in charge of the class and we were highly amused at the well-written text on the blackboard which the children were copying on their slates:

'Jesus loves me. Jesus loves me. Jesus loves me.
You must all cook beer for the Captain.'

I was under the impression that the text referred to me with the flattering promotion and the directive that I should be drowned in beer. I was mistaken. The 'Captain' referred to was the African Salvation officer whose tour of inspection was imminent.

Space does not permit the recounting of the many incidents which occurred on this day-by-day patrol. Each section operated on its own as well as in a combined patrol and I must confine my remarks to the more important incidents.

The supreme test of endurance was undertaken after the Assistant Native Commissioner at Miami, Mr N.E. Brent, met us at the Karoe River, as had previously been arranged. After a conference, we decided that we would send the lorries up to Miami, then along the road to the Catkin Mica Mine, south-west through the Urungwe Reserve to a final destination at Kariana's Kraal on the Badza River. The patrol would footslog across the base of the triangle and rendezvous with the transport at the kraal. There were several problems. It was impossible to obtain any accurate information on the exact whereabouts of the kraal other than that they obtained water from the Badza River, a tributary of the Sanyati. The two lorries and Mr Brent's car would have to travel over a hundred miles whereas our own route was likely to be anything between 35 and 40 miles.

Packs were made up just in case we failed to reach our

objective in the single day and were forced to spend a night in the bush, and at pink of dawn we set out. The routine on the march was to pause for five minutes in every hour and to stop for thirty minutes every four hours so that we could have a wash, if possible, and change socks, brew tea and eat a haversack ration. We kept our spirits up on the journey with swigs of K.B. from our water bottles and our travels were punctuated at regular intervals with minor explosions as the corks popped out of the bottles. We were fortunate in having a few members of the Police Drum and Fife Band in our numbers and they played lively tunes from time to time, which encouraged us to keep going.

At about eight o'clock in the evening we heard the distant sound of the lorry hooters and fired a shot to indicate that we were bang on target and in the vicinity. As we emerged from the bush at the rendezvous, into the headlights of the transport, we made a brave show of our arrival, marching in with our fife band leading the way.

We had made it, and, assuming that the walking pace was three and a third miles per hour and that we had marched solidly for twelve hours since dawn, the distance we had covered to Kariana's kraal from the Karoe River was not far short of 38 miles. We threw ourselves to the ground for a well-earned breather before tackling an excellent supper of stew prepared for us by George Schlachter and Jimmy Powell.

I don't mind admitting that I was 'out' and in no mood for hunting at dawn the next morning, but some of the others of the patrol were and I was awakened by the sound of distant rifle shots. The early birds were demonstrating most aptly that the white man was as tough if not tougher than the local African. Mr Brent, an excellent linguist, recounted our impressive travels to Kariana and Chief Majinga and the tale of our exploits was received with many exclamations of 'Hau Hau!' And 'Are these men majohnnies'.

We had certainly earned a day's rest for a clean-up, washing of clothes and other chores. That night we were treated to a display of tribal dancing and a singsong by inmates of Kariana's kraal and neighbouring kraals under Chief Majinga.

Picture the scene. A full moon, a ring of camp fires lighting up the trees, the shadowy huts in the distance and the faces of the men of the patrol as they lounged on their blankets, replete after an excellent meal of tender Impala steaks.

On came the dancers – men and women in their motley attire, no self-consciousness, all movement and rhythm in the dust thrown up by their stamping feet. Then came the singing. The men on one side and the women on the other, in two ranks facing inwards. After a shrill *puru rudza* greeting by the women – a carrying sound made by exhaling through rounded lips, beaten rapidly by the fingers to obtain a trilling effect – the females sang in a high-pitched minor key:

'*A na mambo a na enzaro.*'

To which the deep throated basses of the men would reply:

'*E yoh ... E yoy ... A na mambo a na enzero ... E yoh ... E yoy.*'

Then more *puru rudza* and a repetition of the whole until one came to be almost hypnotised by the tune and the body movements of the singers.

And what did it all mean? Literally – *The white man has nothing to do – loud cheers.* In other words, we were not on business and were relaxing so they were free to do the same.

Then came a song of praise for their Chief, Majinga. The men and women formed a large circle and, with much stamping of the feet, hand clapping and bodily contortions, the women, fortissimo and in a minor key, sang '*O Majingo!*' The men replied in their deep bass and then again the women, this time more softly, which the men echoed. And then the entire company, fortissimo diminuendo and with much arm raising and feet stamping: *~Ah he yah ... Ah he yah ... Majingo...*

The rhythm and the movement became so infectious that I readily gave permission for the men to join in and we did so with no loss of face and to the obvious enjoyment of the Africans. In passing, I sometimes give a demonstration of the concert performed for us at Kariana's to my own banjo accompaniment and no one has thrown me out yet.

With the patrol over we disbanded at Sinoia and each of us went our separate ways. The Askari returned to Depot and took with them their precious little Bantam cock known as 'Four-by-Two', a present from Chief Majinga which they had adopted as their mascot. The bird was so named because, when let out of his basket at any stopping place, his number one duty would be to seek out the largest cock in the vicinity and beat the very daylights out of him before finding time to appease the 'inner man'. Had anyone suggested that 'Four-by-Two' should find his way into a cooking pot, a mutiny would have been provoked!

Despite the passage of the years, I can still remember the

names of all the European members of the patrol but one:

Sergeant A.M. Cook (Chuku), Corporals Rippon, Tigar and 'Paddy' Nagle, Troopers Jack Hoddinott, Ken Francis, 'Micky' Linton, Mike Quinn and Jack Start.

I wonder how many of these splendid chaps are alive today?

Several months later, Charles Bullock, himself an ex-police-man, had this to say in an official report on the value of the patrol:

> The Police patrol, while operating in a perfectly peaceable manner, demonstrated in no uncertain way that the Government had at its disposal forces capable of swift action in maintaining authority anywhere in the country.

It had been a happy patrol. We had been sent to do a job with the minimum of 'bull' and it seems that we had achieved all that we had set out to do, the good name of the Corps being upper-most in our minds at the time.

Captain Surgey and Corporal Nagle crossing the Sanyati

Crossing a drift

Another drift in the Urungwe Reserve

Thornycroft lorries leaving Sinoia. Tpr. Hoddinott on hood of left lorry

Askari on the left, European members on the right, drivers far right

Parade at Majinga's Kraal. (L/R) Cook, Tigar, Quin, Francis, Linton
Captain Surgey in front. Asst. N.C. Brent's car on right

Loading up at
Majinga's Kraal

1930s

REMINISCENCES

Donovan Anderson Newton
Trooper (3180) British South Africa Police

I met a man with a strong Oxford accent who had served in the B.S.A.P. and he told me tales of his experiences and exploits in Rhodesia, this really fired my imagination and got me thinking. I immediately wrote to the Staff Officer, B.S.A. Police, Salisbury and offered myself for attestation. I received a prompt reply and then sent off the required documents together with a reference from the local Magistrate and his recommendations as to my fluency in Zulu. I was duly accepted and received a rail warrant and so set out on my three-day journey to Salisbury.

It was a wearisome journey through the old Bechuanaland and Rhodesia and I finally arrived at the Salisbury Railway Station at about 10.00 a.m. on a Saturday morning. In the road behind the station stood a taxi and I enquired of the driver the whereabouts of the Police Training School. He replied that it was too far to walk, so I hired him to take me there.

On arrival, I found that everyone was getting ready to pack up for the weekend. A Day Corporal, on my enquiring, pointed me in the direction of a very large man rigged out in spurs, leggings and an R.S.M. badge. I approached him nervously, removed my hat and introduced myself. His quick reply was:

'Newton, did you bring that car in here?'

I replied, 'Yes, Sir.'

'Well, get it to hell out of here, this is a Police Barracks, not a Taxi Rank.'

I immediately paid the taxi off.

R.S.M. Jock Douglas of great fame (1228 James Fife Douglas) called me to him after the taxi episode and took me to a room with shelves holding blankets and instructed me to take three, then pointed me to some barrack rooms and told me to make myself comfortable, he would see me on Monday. I watched various squads of recruits on parade in front of the barracks having their rifles inspected by Inspector Walker (1344 Robert Walker) who had just won the Kings Medal at Bisley in England for shooting.

A coloured man by the name of William who was employed as a mule driver took me to the Salisbury Railway Station in a mule wagon to fetch my trunk and other luggage.

My medical examination was conducted by Dr Huggins, later to become Prime Minister of Southern Rhodesia and then, as Lord Malvern, the first Prime Minister of the Federation of Rhodesia and Nyasaland.

I settled down to training, which I found very hard. Most of the recruits were from Regiments such as the Scots Guards, Irish Dragoons, Queens Bays, Scots Greys and even the Cameron Highlanders and were perfection personified at their drill. Discipline was strict and I, of course, a friendless green-horn. The musketry course was first class but mistakes and awkwardness were never overlooked or allowed to pass without a cursing reprimand.

The day we took the oath and signed on (5th April, 1930), the R.S.M., Jock Douglas, told us that if we were not totally dedicated, not to sign on and then added, 'When you sign that paper, we can and will do anything we like to you, except put you in the family way!!!'

We signed on and, for me, a really hard time began. I could not do P.T., head springs, handsprings and the wooden horse work, having never seen it before, but I persevered and was very good by the end of training. I eventually could do a handspring on the tarred road in my army boots. Horsemanship and equitation were different, I was outstanding right away and once I had learned 'knees on the saddle, heels down', the army style of riding, I was almost an expert.

The Instructors were all from British Regiments and gave me a hard time. I was so 'bawled out' on one occasion by our P.T. Instructor that I heard Captain Onyett (1053 Harry Thomas Onyett) ask our Troop Sgt Major Hampton (2028 Harold Cuthbert Hampton) what sort of rookie I was. His reply was, 'One of my best, Sir,' so I did have some friends after all!

A diminutive Mashona named Munetsi was my batman and brought me tea at reveille and kept my saddlery in tip-top condition.

I was rather unlucky with horses, my first mount was *Cromwell*, the Regiment's best jumper. His normal rider was Sgt Simpson (2074 Joseph Gordon Simpson) who was on his five months' leave in England and by luck I was given *Cromwell*. He was a free jumper and I got over the hurdles without mishap, except for a reprimand for jerking his mouth. Horsemanship and Equitation was at a very high level and we were lectured daily on Riding, Horses and their care, Veterinary, the lot.

Sgt Simpson returned from England and took over his horse and I, of course, had to take one of the leftovers. *Karoo* was my next horse which could not jump or do anything else. I was allowed to parade with a riding switch and had great trouble in all exercises, especially in the riding school which was walled in so that the horses could not see out and had cotton strewn on the ground to save us from hurt when we tumbled. Here we rode bareback, without stirrups and did a lot of jumping and having to salute as we took the hurdles. I found it much easier to take a hurdle bare-back as there were no stirrups to throw one up. I revelled in it all.

Trooper Say, (3177 John Say) a Scots Guardsman, had a spill in the riding school and was knocked unconscious for some minutes and I remember gazing down at his eyes, which were wide open and hearing Captain Onyett saying, 'Say, say', as he also gazed down at him.

We used to ride out to Gun Kopje and do mounted rifleman training (M.R.T.). We were Rhodesia's first line of defence and had Vickers Bertha machine guns mounted on horses. *Karoo*, my horse, was expelled from the Troop and was relegated to carry a machine gun. I was now given *Jumbo*, the biggest nag in our stables. He was so lazy that when he heard the command 'halt' he would immediately stop dead in his tracks.

I was so fit at this stage of my training, I could vault into the saddle with my rifle, which we always carried in a gun bucket behind our right knee or in our hands at any pace faster than a walk. Every morning I used to practise with *Jumbo* whilst waiting to 'fall in', much to the amusement of our R.S.M.

We were often given surprise orders. There were tin sheds at each of the ranges at the rifle range and Sgt Major Hampton would say, 'The first man and horse into that, the best – go.' At other times we would be a mile or so from the butts at the rifle range and he would say, 'The first man to the range and back with some target marking paper, the best – go.' What a race these would turn out to be. There were dry dongas in our path and I did not ever see a horse balk at them – they took them in their stride. I used to ride No. 2 to a man from the Horse Artillery in England called Bellairs (3171 Edward E. James

Bellairs), whose father was a parson in the C. of E. I would leap off my horse which he would then hold, run into the butts, snatch a piece of target paper, mount and we were off knee to knee.

A film unit once came to make a film of us doing 'Pursuit Action' on the range. In this you did not put the second rein over the horse's head but carried it over your elbow and started before the 500 yard range, galloping at full speed between ranges, leaping off and firing two live rounds at the targets. It was gallop, leap off, fire, mount and off again. If you displeased the Troop Sgt Major, the punishment was; off your horse, hand him over to someone else, unsaddle him, then take rifle and saddle and footslog it back to the barracks, miss your breakfast and shave for the first parade. It never happened to me!

We had various parades. The King's Birthday was a gala day and the Governor, Sir H. Rodwell, came and opened our new canteen building and he later had dinner at the Officers' Mess. During the proceedings, I remember a battle royal between two drunken troopers who were bashing each other and had to be put into the cells by the Provost Sgt Stephens (3116 Charles Stephens).

Our Musketry subject took six months to complete and I was the only one to be a Marksman with a Revolver, although there were plenty of Marksmen with rifle shooting.

Once a week, our horses had to go down the jumping lane. It was a race, like a dip-tank with bars on both sides and interspersed with solid stone walls. If a horse did not clear them, it was hurt. Our stirrups were crossed over the saddle, the reins tied to the bridle and the horses kraaled at the start. Then each man led his horse to the start and let go. Stock whips were cracked and the horse went tearing down the race and over the solid hurdles. The horses loathed it and fought to escape, becoming wild-eyed and fighting mad to avoid being put into the kraal. On one occasion, Trooper Hewings' (2953 William Hewings) horse tried to leap out and pushed him against the bars with its chest against his and injured him badly.

We were eventually passed out and entrained to the various districts in which we were to serve. I was sent to Bulawayo as I had previously taken an oral Sindebele examination and, on passing out, received ten pounds.

It was quite sad saying goodbye to friends with whom you had been in trouble and under stress. We bought our Sgt Major a couple of bottles of whisky and wanted to take the R.S.M. out to dinner in Salisbury. A deputation went to his house with the invitation. At first he refused, saying that he had been invited to a dinner by a squad once before and then, as no one had any money, he finished up by paying for the whole lot! His wife, however, encouraged him and said, 'Go with them, Jock, I'll take you down in the car and fetch you later.' What a boisterous party it turned out to be! We ended up by signing our names on his stiff shirt. I wonder whether he kept it? I think it was ruined for any future wear.

From Bulawayo, which I disliked, I was sent to Inyati. It was a forty-mile ride and I was to meet Webb half-way and swap horses with him. He was late and I had to sleep out at the Bembesi River. It was very dry and quite pleasant sleeping with my saddle for a pillow. I arrived at Inyati the next day.

Inyati was all patrols duty. I had No. 2 Section, which was visiting farms. During one of my patrols I came across the Campbell-Watts, whom I later discovered were relatives of mine. Dr Campbell-Watts' wife, who was an Anderson, asked me who my father was and then informed me that she and I were cousins! The ground for Scotsville School in Pietermaritzburg was given to Miss Anderson, who was a schoolteacher, by Dr Campbell-Watts, to be used for the purpose of a school.

At Inyati I was commended by the Commissioner for 'patrol mileage.' Each patrol horse was expected to do 20 miles per day or 600 per month. On long patrol, i.e. when you slept out, you always carried a .303 in a rifle bucket and ammo in your bandolier, which was part of your uniform and worn across the chest.

I had to serve a summons on the Manager of Blackwater Ranch, which was exactly 49 miles from Inyati. I left at 6.00 a.m. and on arrival at Blackwater, I found no one at home, so put the summons on the kitchen table, instructing the servants to draw the Boss's attention to it. I would normally have stayed there but it stormed and I turned for home in pouring rain and arrived at Inyati Police Camp at 6.00 a.m. the next morning. During the night of my ride home, with the rain still pelting down, I had to open a gate and received a terrific electric shock. Lightening must have struck the fence. I saw flashes and heard thunder whilst I was getting over the shock. On reporting back, Sgt le Neve Forster (1493 Sydney le Neve Forster) said, 'Newton, let me have your report NOW.' He was a real 'so and so' and had added Forster to his family name, because the family of 'le Neve' were mixed up in a famous murder trial in England.

I patrolled the Shangani Reserve in the dry season for three months and often watched elephants bathing in Lake Alice on the Gwampa River. I shot great knob-nosed geese to eat and in the spring let my horse *Blesbok* graze on the lovely green grass. He never left my camp and revelled in the freedom. I used to buy native monkey nuts for him and also boil linseed once a week. When available I would buy mealies from Africans and then soak them before feeding him. The only record of my labours was a patrol diary, which was sent to the Commissioner for his perusal – hence my commendation for 'patrol mileage'. I also cleaned and weeded the Allan Wilson Memorial on the Shangani River where the battle in 1893 was fought and all those brave men perished.

'Whisky' Burman, the owner of the Braemar Ranch at Inyati had trading stores in the Reserve and they were the homes of the only whites, who were rather strange and lonely people who had gone 'native'. There were also Tsetse fly trappers who were very eccentric and did a job for the Government that no one else would do. We patrolled on foot when we came to a fly belt, which we would recognise by the lack of the black inhabitants. You could travel a day without seeing a human being. Horses were unknown to most reserve dwelling Africans and they held them in awe. I remember coming to a kraal and heard a youth tell younger children that the horse (*biza*) I was riding, was very vicious and dangerous and could kill with a blow of its hoof.

We used to patrol right up to the Gwaai River and Lupani Hotel, which was half-way to Victoria Falls. I arrived there once when a member of the owner's family had just died and was buried in a bedroom cupboard for lack of a coffin. The husband, of game hunting fame, died of blackwater fever and his wife carried on running the hotel. I have been told that people of the same name are still there.

My best adventure in the Shangani was the pursuit of a gun runner, 'Van', who traded firearms to the locals. When he was discovered, he made for the reserve, which was silly as anyone 'white' stood out like a sore thumb! I was sent to bring him in. He set off in a three ton lorry but towards the end of the chase abandoned it, leaving just enough fuel to get back to civilisation should he get away. I sent my horse back with askaris to Lonely

Mine and I finished up a day behind him on foot. He kept going north and I always knew where he slept from information from the local Africans. He became ill with malaria and now veered towards the south. My break finally came when an African told me that Van would sleep the night at a certain kraal and sent a coloured girl to guide me there. When Van arrived in the evening, I was already sitting under a tree waiting for him. On seeing me he said, 'I have been a terrible fool and now I am sick.' We trekked to his lorry and finally a week later arrived at Lonely Mine. Van was sent to hospital under guard.

It was here that I got abscesses in my ears, through sleeping in the rain and general exposure. Dr Jacob Liltz gave me the option of going to hospital or staying at the Lonely Police Camp. He said that if I attended hospital and they touched my ears with a syringe, they would burst my ear drums. I stayed at camp and had sand bags put in the oven to heat and throughout the night kept changing them which helped me to recover to some degree, but they never actually came right for more than a year.

One other event at Inyati comes to mind. The son of a world famous Lord, Baden-Powell (Arthur Robert Peter Baden-Powell, 3383), joined us from England. He was known as 'The Hon. John'. As I recall, we had another 'Honourable' in the Force, the third son of a Lord – both real 'gentlemen'. I was not partial to the 'Hon. John' and for some reason or other I was detailed to take him on his first patrol; why I still don't know! My patrol detail consisted of some horses, a pack mule, three African Police armed with .45 Elephant guns and a map of the area, which had been made up and added to by Troopers like myself (very good they were, too!). We went to the Gwampa River area where lions normally roamed. On our second camp, I slept among the Askaris for protection. He asked why and I told him that I had it on good authority that a lion will always take a black man in preference to a white and also four or five rifles were better than one for protection. He scoffed at this idea. At sundown, the lions saw our fire and started to roar, making our horses and mule snort and the dogs nearly push us into the fire. Then all was silent and I knew exactly what would happen next. The lions, having seen the fire and being upset, would come closer silently to see what was going on. When quite close and satisfied of no particular danger to themselves, they would let out the most terrible roar, frightening the life out of everyone. The hair on the back of my neck used to stand up and my dogs would try to get under the blankets with me. This indeed happened and was enough to get to the 'Hon. John', and he picked up his bedding and reluctantly joined us. He did not stay more than three years in the B.S.A.P. He was a real pain in the neck!

I decided that I would leave the 'bush' station. We had quite a few deaths from blackwater and enteritis, and the number of suicides was appalling. I was then stationed at Victoria Falls for a short while and became very friendly with Transvaal school teachers who used to come up for short holidays. They taught me a lesson or two! American tourists were quite amazing. If one said to you, 'Police Officer, where is the nearest "drop in", it meant he wanted a post box!' A young girl once looked me over and said to her father, 'Paw, ain't he cute.'

Trooper Newton left the B.S.A.P. on 16th September 1934.

The historic photograph on the opposite page, taken for the 50th Anniversary of the British South Africa Police, is notable in that the service of the members depicted span a total of 74 years of the Force's 91 year history.

The veterans seated were attested in 1889, while B.G. Spurling retired as Commissioner in 1963. In addition to the then Commissioner, Col. Morris, four future Commissioners were present, Messrs Ross, Hickman, Jackson and Spurling.

Col. A.J. Tomlinson joined in 1894 and, when he retired in 1926, was the last serving member who took part in the Jameson Raid.

BRITISH SOUTH AFRICA POLICE:

PAST AND PRESENT. JUBILEE, 1890.1940. SALISBURY, 13 SEPTEMBER, 1940.

Seated—Pioneer Police (left to right): A. J. Mallet-Veale, Esq.; Capt. H. J. Hare; Major W. Howard, D.S.O.; M. E. Weale, Esq.; Lieut.·Colonel C. H. F. Divine, D.S.O.; C. F. Bertram, Esq.; J. L. Crawford, Esq.; J. A. Palmer, Esq.; R. Carruthers Smith, Esq.Standing (left to right): S/M. J. Flockhart, ex-B.S.A.P.; R.S.M. G. A. Tantum; S/M. T. A. Jacobs, Det. Sgt. D. H. Greengrass, M.M.; Det. Insp. W. V, Bond; Insp. D. Graham; Det. Sgt. J. E. Chubbock; Capt. A. S. Hickman; Sgt. C. W. Buncombe; S/M. R. Stoker; S/M. G. W. T. Ashwin; Insp. A. C. Vowles; Major J. E. Ross; Colonel A. J. Tomlinson (1894), Major H. Bugler; Major J. S. Bridger; Major P. J. Bagshawe, C.M.G., M.B.E. (1896); Capt. R. P. Derhant; Lieut. G. C. Rogers; Colonel J. S. Morris, C.B.E. (Inspector General); Lieut. B. G. Spurling; Major H. Rochester; Lieut. G. S. A. Rolfe; Major W. J. Philips, O.B.E.; Lieut. H. Jackson; S/M. L. G. Gaylord; S/M. A. J. S. McLeod; S/M. W. H. Halls; Insp. L. B. Goodall; Capt. E. T. Fox, C.B.E.; Major R. Hamilton, O.B.E.; Sgt. W. G. Leyland; Capt. J. F. Douglas, ex-B.S.A.P.; Lieut. C. W. H. Thatcher; S/M. J. G. Simpson, D.C.M.

1940s

MILITARY TO CIVIL

John Berry
5584, British South Africa Police

The 1940s was a decade of major significance for the B.S.A. Police, starting with the declaration of war in 1939. The Southern Rhodesia Government had been preparing for this and, in 1936, had appointed Col. Morris as Commandant-General of the S.R. Forces, both military and the Police. As such he carried the main burden of the country's preparation for war, until July 1940, when the command was split and Col. Morris resumed command of the B.S.A. Police with the designation of Inspector-General. The Government paid tribute to the way in which he had handled the joint commands.

During the war, a number of members, 138 all told, had been seconded for service in the Occupied Territories in North Africa. (See No.7 in the Series, *Military Operations outside Southern Rhodesia in World Wars I and II.*) This was a significant proportion of the European establishment of the Force and, as recruitment had ceased, the work of policing the country fell on a much-diminished number of men. To fill the vacuum, a Police Reserve was established and also the Southern Rhodesia Women's Auxiliary Police Service, and these units gave outstanding and vital service during the war.

Mechanised transport had largely taken over from the horse and much greater efficiency was achieved. A Recce Unit was established, using locally-built armoured cars, crewed by Police Reserve.

African Police uniforms, pay and conditions were greatly improved and greater use made of them.

A recruitment drive was started immediately after the war, mainly in the United Kingdom, to bring the Force up to strength. A notable intake of 94 recruits arrived aboard the *Alcantara* in 1946. Due to lack of space in Depot and shortage of trained instructors, these were put through a training programme of only a few weeks and then sent out to stations.

Fortunately, all had seen service in the War and were accustomed to discipline.

Also in 1946, the Mundy Commission was established to report on all aspects of the Police and resulted in much improved service conditions. It also recognised that the Force must move to being a completely civil one. Despite this, it was only in the early 1950s that military titles were phased out and even then those who already had them were allowed to retain them, albeit frozen at their current level.

In 1947, strikes by African workers in Bulawayo were a portent of the things to come and a future nationalist leader, Joshua Nkomo, began making his presence felt. The Police response to the unrest created by the strikers required new methods of operation in these situations and much was learned. It was found then and in succeeding decades that a Police Reserve was essential.

Police Recce Unit armoured cars in the 1940s.
They were locally made. Typical Force Orders of late 'Forties

PROMOTIONS

No. 3904, Const. Marnoch, Salisbury Town to 2/Sergeant, 1.6,47.

No. 3622, D/2/Sgt. Hodges, C.I.D., Bulawayo, to D/1/Sergeant, 1·10.47.

No. 3535, D/2/Sgt. Lee, C.I.D. Bulawayo, to D/1/Sergeant, 1.10.47.

No. 3675, D/2/Sgt. Grundy, C.I.D., Salisbury, to D/1/Sergeant, 1.10.47.

No. 3729, D/2/Sgt· Barton, C.I.D., Bulawayo, to D/1/Sergeant, 1.10.47.

No. 3761, D/2/Sgt. McDonald, C.I.D. Bulawayo, to D/1/Sergeant, 1.10.47.

ATTACHMENTS

The undermentioned members are attached to the Criminal Investigation Department for six months from dates stated:—

No. 3961, Tpr. Henderson, Gatooma District, to C.I.D. Salisbury, 19·9.47.

No. 4003, Const. Dunbar, Bulawayo Town to C.I.D. Bulawayo, 9.9.47.

No. 4057, Tpr. Ogle, Gwelo District to C.I.D Bulawayo, 11.9.47·

No. 4111, Tpr. Oakley, Victoria District to C.I.D. Bulawayo, 9.9.47.

ATTESTATIONS

The undermentioned for the District Branch for three years at £226 p.a. and posted to Depot, as stated:

No. 4203, Tpr. George Innes Baker, 15.9.47.

No· 4204, Tpr. Ian David Brink, 16.9.47.

No. 4205, Tpr. Derek Nelson Ambrose, 28.9.47.

No. 4206, Tpr. Michael Peter Avery, 28.9.47.

No. 4207, Tpr. William John Barratt, 28.9.47.

No. 4208, Tpr. Peter Harold Bartlett, 28·9.47.

No. 4209, Tpr. Julian Francis Hassard Burkitt, 28.9.47.

No. 4210, Tpr. Brian Probert Chadwick, 28.9.47.

No. 4211, Tpr. Peter William John Curtain, 28.9.47.

No. 4212, Tpr. Thomas Albert Griffith, 28.9.47.

No. 4213, Tpr. Edward Mathew Blagden Hale, 28.9.47.

No. 4214, Tpr. Godfrey Douglas Hodgson, 28.9.47.

No. 4215, Tpr. Arthur William Kennard, 28.9.47.

No. 4216, Tpr. Edward William Kirby, 28.9.47.

No. 4217, Tpr. Peter Schofield, 28.9.47.

No. 4218, Tpr. David Lindsay Smith, 28.9.47.

The undermentioned for the Town Branch for three years from 28.9.47 at £226 p.a. and posted to Depot:—

No. 4219, Const. Stanley Lazenby Bruce.

No. 4220, Const. Michael Edward Diprose.

No. 4221, Const. Ronald Dudley Eames.

No. 4222, Const. Henry George Heywood.

No. 4223, Const. Peter Graham Marshall.

No. 4224, Const. Derrick Robinson.

No. 4225, Const. Ronald Underwood.

DISCHARGES

No. 3556, 2/Sgt. Bayne, Salisbury District, "retirement on gratuity," 30.9.47.

No. 3638, 2/Sgt. Lee, Gwelo, District, "retirement on gratuity," 29.9.47.

CIVIL SERVICE LOWER LAW EXAMINATION RESULTS: PART II

The undermentioned passed the above examination as stated:—

No. 3749, 2/Sgt. Edwards, Salisbury District, 11.6.47.

CIVIL SERVICE NATIVE CUSTOMS AND ADMINISTRATION EXAMINATION RESULTS

The undermentioned passed the above examination as stated:—

No. 3860, 2/Sgt. Payne, Bulawayo District, 13.6.47.

1950s

FALL'S EXCURSIONS

John David 'Gus' Fall
Trooper 4479/5420 British South Africa Police

Some of the following stories have been published, some not. They have been edited in order to place them in chronological order.

STAND TO YOUR HORSES

I was talking to old Smudger the other day about the military employment of horses. He still thinks that Mounted Infantry are a good thing. Smudger was our equitation instructor ~ so he would! I can still remember the day we arrived in Depot and he bounced into the barrack room, announced that he was Trooper Smith and that he was our course instructor. The next day he was promoted to Lance Sergeant and tasked with giving us riding lessons. Well, in a way, it might be more accurate to say that we gave him his because we were his first squad ~ Tony Butler, Mike Oates, Buck Telfer, Bill Neale, Taffy Phillips, Chris Moon and me. Very small and select squad, we were.

Claude De Lorme gave us our foot drill and 'Bundu' Charlie Woodgate instructed on musketry ~ not that we needed much of either because, apart from Taffy and Chris, we had all done our National Service. Stan Edwards tried to keep us awake with Law and Police.

But Smudger gave us the horsey bit ~ which National Service hadn't touched on. Apart from Buck Telfer, who claimed to have ridden before, the rest of us had never thrown a leg over anything bigger than a Southend donkey. Daresay it looked like it, too. But keen we were. We used to compare saddle sores in the ablutions after the early morning ride.

I well remember the morning I asked Smudger a perfectly innocent question about my surcingle. Getting a bit tatty it was and I reckoned it was high time for a bit of kit exchange. I never discovered whether my tone was less than conciliatory or that Smudger had awoken after a hard night in the Mess but as soon as we reached the bottom paddock it was crossed stirrups and forty-five minutes of non-stop troop drill. I took the prize for bruises and abrasions that morning. RH *Kismet* was a good nag though. Used to kick the daylights out of anything smelling his tail so we were consigned to the rear of the ride and that meant no decisions had to be made and we just followed in the wake of the man ahead. Not that any serious decision making was ever necessary. The quads knew the drill better than any of us and it was all we could do to apply the aids ~ to Smudger's satisfaction ~ before the evolution had been completed.

I mentioned what a small and select recruit squad was honoured with my presence. Like most post-war recruits, I suppose we were fairly mature but in many respects we were a pretty unsophisticated bunch ~ particularly in our tastes for entertainment.

It wasn't surprising really, coming from war-time Britain where the general level of available entertainment was austere to say the least of it, even until the early fifties.

One of our most popular venues of amusement in Depot was, needless to say, the Wet Canteen which Don Lane ran on the ground floor of the Regimental Institute. On Saturday and Sunday evenings before supper, particularly after a match, the Troops' Canteen rang with raucous song. Dicky Hazelhurst was choir-master simply because he had the loudest voice and the most compelling personality. Such classic arias as The One-Eyed Reilly, Kafoozleum (my own particular favourite) and The Lobster Song and others of similar ribaldry were sung with enormous gusto and enjoyment.

Among our more ardent supporters was Clancy Pickard (not Bert, the ex-Life Guardsman). He was never christened Clancy but won the title because he was particularly fond of Clancy Lowered the Boom of which he alone knew all the verses and which was invariably called for during the course of a session. There were those in our company who knew the choruses of practically all the music hall numbers of the era, songs such as My Old Man, Little Dolly Daydream, She was a Dear Little Dickybird and Any Old Iron and these too were rarely excluded from our repertoire.

Proof of our vocal talents, so carefully nurtured in Don Lane's Academy of Music, came some time after I left Depot but while I was still in Salisbury. About a dozen of us attended an Old Time Music Hall down town, having stopped off at the Queens

Hotel to lubricate our tonsils. Then we paid our admission fee and took over the back two rows of the hall.

Obviously Dennis Sherringham would have been there, plus Clancy Pickard and Johnny Yeoman and the other old stalwarts. The performance opened with the pianist playing a sort of overture ~ a selection of old favourites. They were old favourites and the occupants of the two last rows were highly delighted as recognition dawned. Not being shy, we didn't wait for the soubrettes and performing gentry to lead us ~ we'd sung them often enough without invitation and there seemed to be no reason why we shouldn't burst forth on this occasion. The remainder of the audience exhibited a degree of surprise at first but then, as now, where the Corps will lead, others will follow. The evening warmed up rapidly and very nicely. Later we were given to understand that this enthusiasm caused some apprehension among the performers who were not accustomed to such vigorous support so early in the evening. Indeed, one of the young ladies was moved to remark, after we had accompanied her through her first chorus, that she smelled policemen in the audience. We loudly cheered this percipient remark and redoubled our efforts. The essence of good live Music Hall was, after all, audience participation ~ and so we participated. A good time was had by all and I doubt whether many subsequent shows were quite as lively.

As I mentioned, Stan Edwards was our Law and Police instructor. Stan regaled us with examples many and varied of the villainy of the two arch-criminals, Tembo and Zuze. Sometimes Tembo was the victim, sometimes Zuze, and sometimes they acted in concert to perpetrate their nefarious plans. But sure as eggs, one or other was bound to figure in Stan's repertoire of miscellaneous offences. He was, of course, a district policeman, and he imbued in us a burning desire for a posting to Sipolilo ~ an ambition which, alas, I never achieved. Naturally, we all put in for postings to district though.

Before we passed out of Depot, however, we had to obtain driving licences for both truck and motorcycle. Claude de Lorme was appointed instructor and, as nearly as I can remember, we had four hours tuition on each vehicle. I had ridden a motorcycle before so was quickly dismissed from the parade. The four-wheel vehicle scene was rather more complex and the first hour of instruction was spent careering round the Hard Square (not then cluttered up with police reserve vehicles, fortunately) learning to change gear. The second hour consisted of a venture on to the Borrowdale Road, the third let us loose in the Avenues and finally the unsuspecting jay walkers in First and Second Streets received our attention.

The following day we went into town and were given our licences ~ and our exit visas from Depot. At least, this was the general idea but I see from my file of Force Orders (having kept all those in which I received a mention) that Butler, Oates and myself were posted from Depot w.e.f. 10.1.50; Phillips w.e.f. 13.1.50, and Moon, Neal and Telfer w.e.f. 16.1.50. This was odd because of the whole squad only Buck Telfer claimed to have held a driving licence but his late departure indicates that he had failed his driving test at the first attempt. The fact that I was lucky enough to earn my licence at the first go should not be interpreted as a measure of my driving ability. Subsequent events indicated the contrary.

CYCLES AND SUBURBIA

As we had all applied for the District Branch, we were naturally posted to Town. Taffy Phillips was exiled to Gwelo but the rest of us went to Salisbury Urban and reported to Superintendent Bill Walker, the Officer Commanding at Baker Avenue. Then we were seen by the Town Inspector who told us to go out and purchase bicycles as we would soon be in need of them. I took myself off to Messrs Fulton and Evans and bought one on hire purchase ~ well, extended credit really. Notwithstanding the fact that I was a member of the B.S.A. Police, the manager was not terribly anxious to give me credit. Changed days, indeed.

Not only did I need my cycle to get from Depot, where we were still living, to the Baker Avenue Charge Office, but it was one of the 'appointments' with which we paraded. And, what's more, if there happened to be a spare constable on duty, a cycle patrol was included on the duty roster. The final indignity was to be issued with a watch-clock which we jolly well had to punch at the appropriate points! Charge office duties were hardly remarkable, apart from the fact that I wore my pith helmet for the first and last time whilst so employed. The occasion was the Opening of Parliament when I paraded in gaberdines and helmet and traditional splendour. For the rest of my service the helmet reposed in its bag. Only once after that did I see a helmet actually being worn on duty ~ ordinary duty, that is. I went to

Lundi Pools to see the hippos and stayed overnight at the Lundi Hotel. A district policeman drove up in an open four-by-four (Army surplus, I suppose) and he was actually wearing his pith helmet.

Foot patrols round Salisbury were little more exciting than charge office duties ~ except for one night. I was in the immediate vicinity of the old Princes Cinema sometime after midnight and everything was quiet. Then, standing under the canopy above the main entrance, I heard a scrabbling sound from on high. Calmly I checked my baton, torch and whistle, moved noiselessly from under the canopy and looked up. With a lithe spring, as of a tiger, I jumped backwards all of six feet without touching the ground. An enormous rhinoceros beetle lost its footing on the canopy and thudded to the pavement at my feet. That was another incident which was never recorded in my notebook.

After only six weeks I had the good fortune to be posted to Avondale. The Member-in-Charge was Sergeant Butch Buckley and the European strength consisted of Buck Buchanan, John March and Alec ... Alec was one of the most pleasant fellows I ever had the pleasure of meeting during my service. He'd been a major in the Ghurkas and had collected a couple of M.C.s during the war. I don't think Alec ever orientated himself to peacetime because he was in the habit of drinking gin out of a pint mug ~ neat! This meant that there were the odd occasions on which he reported for duty in an unfit condition. Once or twice, when Alec was on night shift (we had one man on from four o'clock until midnight), I stood in for him after doing my own eight-to-four.

One evening, having returned from a rather tiring rural patrol, I decided that Alec would get by on his own. But he didn't. The rest of us left him about five o'clock sitting pensively over the charge office fire and much later, he apparently called out the African driver, A/C Shupiko, I think, to drive him round the beats. At midnight it was the practice to convey the correspondence, the court roll and the deposit sheets down to Baker Avenue before making for Depot and bed. Alec took the station truck on this occasion (Butch never minded, especially if the weather was inclement) and duly handed in the relevant documents at the Main Station. The Charge Office Sergeant, noticing that Alec was hardly in any condition to drive, asked him for the truck keys and offered to get a detail to drive him home. Alec refused and the sergeant went through to speak to the Duty Sub-Inspector. Both emerged from the station to witness the Avondale truck being reversed into one of the C.I.D. cars parked outside. Poor Alec was placed under arrest, charged with being drunk in charge, fined £20 and subsequently discharged. Which was a very great pity.

When I arrived at Avondale, Buck Buchanan ~ in his wisdom ~ decided that it would be inconvenient to have two Johns on the station and I was politely informed that henceforth, for all practical purposes, I would be 'Gus'. Why on earth he chose that particular name, I don't know ~ I fancy he thought it suited me. Come to think of it, it must have done. Certainly I was known by no other name (in polite company) during my service.

Butch, being an ex-district man, tried to run his station on district lines which meant that there was only one member on duty on Saturday afternoons and Sundays. This was good stuff ~ it did away with the tiresome business of having a rest day in the middle of the week. Butch also had a thing about kaffir beer and a beer raid was scheduled for practically every Saturday morning.

What happened was that instead of going off at midnight, the Friday night detail stayed at the station dozing until about five o'clock. He then sallied forth in a three-tonner, borrowed from Baker Avenue, with all the African police volunteers he could muster. As these expeditions were regarded as a good lark, we were never short of volunteers. Then we would descend upon the compound of some suspect farm, search it for beer, seize the beer and the illegal brewer and then move on to the next farm. When the truck was full of victims and their exhibits we would return to the station, the raiding detail would type up the necessary documents and then go off to bed.

Naturally the farmers receiving our attentions used to get furious and although I couldn't see why then, I can certainly do so now. There were several farms on which we could bank for a good haul and we used to bust them unmercifully. Our actions must have played havoc with labour relations but beer-brewing was against the law and ~ *fiat justitia, coelam ruat* (which, freely interpreted, meant 'We'll convict the blighter even if the roof falls in!').

But all in all, Butch was a good Member-in-Charge and popular with the Avondale public so our forays for beer didn't harm our P.R. image too much.

Talking of beer, perhaps I should explain that in those days the Avondale section included Mount Pleasant on the one side, as far out as M'gutu Farm on the Mazoe Road, Lowdale Farm to the east, everything up to Nyabira on the Lomagundi Road and down past Kirkman's on the Old Gatooma Road. With such a huge area, we had plenty of farms to choose from. Mabelreign was still an open vlei north of Meyrick Park and I well remember chasing a grass fire across what is now the suburb of Mabelreign.

The Act provided (still does, for all I know) that anyone could be called upon to assist in extinguishing a grass fire and on this particular occasion I had a span of locals pressed into service. As the fire progressed we came across a 44-gallon drum of beer which some thoughtful peri-urbanite had left in the veld ready for the following weekend ~ far enough from his hut to elude the vigilance of the Alcoholics Anonymous of the Avondale section. The fire had exposed the drum to view. For the time being I told my conscripts to leave the drum alone but when the fire had eventually been extinguished, I rallied my assistants and returned to the prize. Tasting it first, to make sure that the beer was fully matured, I invited my blackened crew to refresh themselves after their labours. Which then they naturally did, with right good will.

During that rainy season my lack of driving expertise caught up with me. One night I received a report that a motorcyclist had been seen lying next to his machine near what is now Greencroft. I asked the motorist making the report what he had done about it. Nothing ~ he'd been in too much of a hurry to report the accident to the authorities! Grabbing the African constable, I jumped into the station truck ~ a Ford Pilot saloon with a box body grafted on to the back. It was quite a nippy vehicle although the V-8 engine had seen some pretty rough service. It was raining like fun but out into the night sped the fearless 'Gus' on his errand of mercy.

The municipality area ended at Sophia Mansions ~ and so did the full tar road. From there to Karoi stretched the Lomagundi Road in all the magnificence of two narrow strips. Pressing on regardless, I misjudged the strips, skidded frantically and executed a neat 180 degree turn, coming to rest in the ditch facing the way I had come. By the time we had replaced the truck on the road and then gone to the scene of the 'accident', some considerable time had elapsed. We searched up and down the verge for the injured motorcyclist but if he had ever been anything more than a figment of my informant's imagination, he had long since recovered and taken himself off. The following night it was still raining and I received a report of a punch-up taking place at the Quorn Hotel. Again the intrepid lad mounted his trusty truck. Again he boldly approached the municipal boundary ~ only this time, of course, he was forewarned. Not for him a repetition of the miserable fiasco of the previous night. Not much! The truck executed precisely the same manoeuvre as before and by the time I reached the Quorn all signs of violent altercation had evaporated in the haze of alcoholic reconciliation.

MIAMI OR THEREABOUTS

Notwithstanding the delights of serving at Avondale under Butch Buckley, my heart was set in the long grass, not only because Stan Edwards, my Law and Police Instructor, had fed me with the ambition to go to Sipolilo, but Butch had also given me a yen to go to Zaka. Butch told us he had gone to Zaka after a difference of opinion with a warrant officer had ended with Butch handing him a fourpenny one on the hooter. Besides, I hadn't come six thousand miles to hang around the Grand, the Posada or the Palace. I could have done that just as well in Southampton, Leeds, Glasgow or Belfast (I already had, in fact). Imagine then, my delight in being informed that I was being posted to Miami. Of course, I didn't suppose for one moment that this Miami would be anything like Miami, Fla. (I wasn't wrong, either) but what a magnificent name! And best of all, it was the far north ~ apart from Chirundu, of which more, much more, anon.

On to Lomagundi! The R.M.S. bus took me to Karoi, where I found the Trooper-in-Charge, Johnny Worsley, ensconced with three A.P. in a cast-off Post Office pre-fab. and two mud huts. I spent the night with him and the next day the Member i/c Miami, 2/Sgt Eric Collier, sent the truck down to collect me. When I got to Miami, my cup of joy was at last full. The offices were Kimberley brick under thatch, the quarters were brick under corrugated iron and the water supply was brought from the spruit below the camp in a water trailer hauled by two oxen. Gone was the tiresome life of Depot with its 'Dust the tops of your mosquito nets, you men in Bodle Block', gone the effete luxury of the Town Police Hostel, with its fascinating female Mess Caterer. Here was the real B.S.A. Police which I had journeyed so far to join.

And if anyone thinks I am rhapsodising through the roseate haze which time does spread over recollection, I can only say that whether they can credit it or not, this was what brought young men to Africa. Not the Disco or Le Coq D'Or (though I took my girl there too when it first opened), not the climate, cold Castle or anything else but Africa unadorned, and from the sparkle of quartz to the blue-print skirts of the women, I knew I was at last where it was at.

The senior Trooper, Lofty Stokes, was out 'Walking the Valley'. Imagine it. One Trooper and two African Constables with what they thought they would need for the gentle stroll from Kariba Gorge (and it was just a gorge in those days) to the Chewore River mouth. No communications, no re-supply, no transport ~ but whatever bearers they could pin down and hire at a shilling a day. A trooper, I think, was allowed six or eight, the number rising according to rank. Could the heart of man ask for anything more? Well, certainly not me.

Lofty had arranged to rendezvous at the Rekomitje Mission, after he had passed through Chirundu. Johnny Worsley had already preempted the opportunity for a more comfortable trip to the Zambesi and, much to my chagrin, took off in the station truck to collect whatever prisoners, witnesses and exhibits Lofty might have gathered to his bosom. Great was my joy, therefore, when a message got back to us that Johnny had arrived at the Mission all right, but that the following morning, on attempting to start the truck, there had been a horrible grinding noise from the back. The differential was now bone dry and consisted principally of iron filings. Eric borrowed the Native Department truck, an Austin A40 pick-up, and told me to go and bring Johnny back. Nothing loath, off I went and, for the first time, dropped over the Zambesi Escarpment. (Not literally 'dropped', of course.) It was a thrill then and though I have done it many times since, the thrill has yet to wear off. Directions were simple; turn right at the foot of the escarpment and head off through the bush. The track was not quite as well worn as it is now, but it wasn't too difficult to follow, even for a town policeman. But it wasn't a very good track and the ride was a trifle bumpy.

When we reached the Rekomitje River, there was, as per

normal, a distinct absence of water but the dry river-bed had been corded with mopani poles. I stalled the engine trying to mount the far side, but then allowed the pick-up to roll back to the bottom. Getting out to make sure that all four wheels were atop the makeshift causeway, I noticed a streak of oil on the slope. Fearing the worst, I bent down and looked under the pick-up. The sump plug had come out and the slick I had seen was the last of my engine oil moistening the riverbed.

We had passed a kraal about three miles back so I told the constable who was with me to go there, borrow a cycle and ride to Makuti Road Camp where there was a telephone. He was to ring Karoi, ask for a gallon of oil and a new sump plug.

The constable pushed off and I took stock. I had four bottles of Castle (for some unaccountable reason), a tin of pilchards, a tin of peaches and a tin of cream. I had not intended staying long and I knew that Johnny had ample provisions. I also had my rifle and ten rounds and a pair of corduroy slacks. Oh yes, and a camouflage veil.

The flies found me ~ they usually do, especially if you are in a streambed. Their bites stung rather, so I made a fire and lit my pipe hoping that this would discourage them. Far from discouraging them, it merely whetted their appetite. I put on the corduroy bags and crouched over the fire. This was uncomfortably hot and I discovered why. I had burnt a hole in my cords. I abandoned the fire and sat in the pick-up. The flies came in through the open window and bit me some more. I closed the windows ~ and perspired even more profusely than before. I got out of the truck and the flies, who had by this time warmed to their work and had told their friends in the Zambesi Valley about their lucky find, got stuck in again. I was becoming seriously inconvenienced. The camouflage veil was the answer. No, I did not drape it over me and pretend to be a bump on a log, because tsetse flies are much too fly to be taken in by such a flimsy pretence. I closed the door on it so that it hung like a curtain over the open window, and tucked it into the window slot. This afforded a partial degree of ventilation and, thus inspired, I plucked some mopani leaves and stuffed them into the top of the other window, having opened it about two inches. This apparently baffled and nonplussed the flies in that they ceased feeding on me. Night was now falling and to keep my spirits up and assuage my thirst, I opened a very warm bottle of Castle and made on it a frugal repast. The African night enfolded me and I slept.

The next morning I awoke and got out of the pick-up. I looked down and was interested to observe lion spoor traversing my footprints round the vehicle. At least, I have always maintained that it was lion spoor, simply because I never saw any gigantic Great Danes in the Valley. But I am willing to concede that my training in tracking came short on my making a really positive identification. The flies greeted me like a long-awaited Meal on Wheels. Disregarding their impertinences, I made a frugal breakfast off another bottle of warm Castle. In answer to the obvious question ~ why did I not scoff the pilchards ~ I can only say that I did not know how long I was likely to be there, and I proposed to sell my life dearly.

Finding the scenery monotonous, I shouldered my rifle and prospected around. Here I was in the heart of what was reputed to be first-rate game country. Was there not meat on the hoof to be had? Very possibly, but it was not hoofing my way. I did find the kraal to which I had directed the A.C. and there I requested a cup of water. When it was brought I glanced into it and, seeing the matter suspended therein, both animate and inanimate, merely put it to my lips before returning it with profuse thanks. Not much fancying the cold sadza adhering to the nearby pot, I pushed on and slowly made my way back to the truck. Was I too proud to eat cold sadza? Not really. After war-time English rations, you got used to being able to eat almost anything. But, by the same token and with the hardships of National Service, you also got used to making do with very little food for long periods.

Back at the truck, I took the appropriate anti-fly precautions and waited. Approximately twenty-four hours after I had stopped in the river-bed, the welcome sound of a Roads Department three-tonner fell upon my expectant ears. A friendly ganger fitted the new drain plug and poured in a gallon of oil and I went on to the Mission.

On my arrival at the Mission, I was somewhat disappointed to find that there was nobody at home. Johnny Worsley and the missionary had gone with Lofty Stokes to his camp on the river in the missionary's truck. It was a well-known vehicle in those parts and was remarkable for the legend which it bore on the back, 'You will meet God at the end of the road.' Fine if you stayed on the road! But at least here was a kitchen with tea and even milk therein, so I refreshed myself with copious draughts of tea and dined off my own pilchards.

The next morning, Johnny and the missionary returned from their R.V. with Lofty, laden with the spoils of the chase. The missionary, whose name was Martin Uppendahl, was an American with TEAM, and had been a parachutist or commando in the U.S. Army. He habitually toured the bush with a .45 automatic strapped to his thigh.

I had noticed a number of medical textbooks on his shelf and asked if he was a doctor. Not at all, he replied, but when he had first come to the Valley, he had attempted to preach the gospel with only a bible in his hand. He had soon found that if he did not have a bandage and a bottle of pills in his other hand, he had to preach only to the mopani trees. The medical textbooks were to enable him to minister to the physical needs of his scattered flock, which in turn enabled him to inject some spiritual medicine along the way.

Lofty had collected quite a good haul of poachers, illicit weapons, witnesses, exhibits and the like and, when we departed from the Mission, we were fairly laden. Johnny offered to do the driving, which offer I promptly accepted.

All went well until we rejoined the main road and turned left to climb the escarpment. Something had gone wrong with the gear-shift and we could not engage first or second gear. Reversing along the road, Johnny gunned the engine and we flung ourselves at the escarpment. But the escarpment in those days had a road winding upwards in very sharp curves and, laden as we were, it was impossible to maintain sufficient speed in third gear to get up that hill. We rolled back to the bottom.

But Trooper Worsley was a District man, and District men are not easily baffled. He had had quite enough of the Valley for this trip, and so had I. Besides, there was no beer left. It was time for a reversal of fortunes ~ so we did! Turning the truck, Johnny told me to hang out of the near-side (now the off-side) door and give him steering instructions. He couldn't use the rear view mirror because the back was full of *kutundu* destined to appear in Court. And, of course, there was no wing mirror. Up the escarpment we went with me hanging out of the door shouting instructions to Johnny and when we reached the top at last he turned the truck, engaged third gear and we returned home.

After having spent eighty days in the Valley, Lofty was eventually brought home by Eric. My Member i/c obviously didn't trust either Johnny or myself to get there and back without mishap. Lofty was a bit distrait, I thought. He had a touch of what we used to call 'bundu stare'. Well, he was thoroughly entitled to it. He had walked nine hundred miles in that eighty days and had, he claimed, shot twenty-two different kinds of edible game. Daresay he had too. I reckon he had shot just about every kind of edible and inedible game in the Valley. We went round to the local butcher's for a sundowner the night Lofty got back. The butcher was a gentleman by the name of Greenhaigh, who rejoiced in the nickname of 'Spiv'. Lofty didn't say much, but sat in his chair downing beers steadily. After the eighteenth beer (I know it was the eighteenth, because there were eighteen empties by his chair) he stood up, started to say something, and fell flat on his face, out for the count. Eric and I picked him up and carried him away. Eighty days without any re-supply. I reckoned he deserved every drop of his (or rather, Spiv's) beer. Just bear that in mind, will you, the next time your deep-freeze breaks down or the canteen truck doesn't pitch up.

Alas, my sojourn at Miami was all too short. After three months I was posted to Darwendale. What a comedown, after I had crowed over my half-section, Tony Butler, who had only got as far north as Banket. I was even nearer to Salisbury now than he was. Almost suburbia. But I'll tell you about that some other time.

Whilst I was at Miami, I was sent on relief to Chirundu. The Chirundu section consisted of two European details and three A.P. The duties consisted of manning the bridge from 6.00 a.m. until 12 noon, and from 12 noon until 6.00 p.m. From 6.00 p.m. until 6.00 a.m., the bridge was closed. This was before the Federation, before the N.R. Police had a post there and before the pub had been built. There was an Indian store on the Northern Rhodesia side and that was it. The accommodation consisted of the wooden bungalow built for the Bridge Engineer which had been erected on the bluff when the bridge was being built, and another bungalow (where the present Charge Office now stands) which was also the office then. We did not have a Crime Register there. On the rare occasions that a crime was actually reported, an entry was made in the Karoi C.R. When I say that the duties consisted of manning the bridge, I mean that one of us sat in the office and made a note of the registration number of any vehicle crossing the bridge. There was no Immigration or Customs to fool about with. If a wanted vehicle was known to be headed for us, we were told and it was our task to detain the occupants until collected. Occasionally we were given instructions to search a vehicle. Apart from that ~ nothing. The greatest enemy, frankly, was boredom. And, of course, the danger that a conflict of personality would develop between two young men who seldom saw anyone else from 6.00 p.m. until 6.00 a.m. The normal tour at Chirundu, I think, was only six months ~ for obvious reasons. Of course, I didn't do a full tour ~ just a week or two. Talk about an Outpost, that was an outpost with a vengeance. Odd to think of two troopers sitting in their vests, just writing down car numbers. But it didn't seem odd then, it was just part of the job. But I wasn't sorry to get back to Miami.

There was a story about Miami which I've always liked. Miami was, in the days when mica was an important mineral, the principal source of supply. The Grand Parade and The Turning Point were flourishing mines. Why, at one time, there had been a hotel at Miami and the stories about that and the legendary French Marie were worth listening to. Anyway, B.S.A. Police Miami itself was situated on a very rich mica lode and several policemen had wished they could have pegged it. (They did, subsequently, but that is another story.) Anyway, in the camp there was a hole and a big pile of mica clippings. When mica is mined, it comes out in irregular lumps and it is clipped with a pair of shears to make it into nice regular 'books'. The price varies according to the grade and colour of the mica and the size of the 'book'. So around a mica mine, you will always find a pile of clippings. And, as I say, there was a hole and lots of mica clippings in the camp. It seems that during the war, when the manpower shortage was acute, Corporal Lofty Lloyd had been Member i/c Miami (the same Lofty Lloyd who had been mess caterer when I was in Depot). In those days, officers often did surprise inspections which were just what the name suggests. The officer pitched up unannounced. On one occasion, the SDO rocked up at Miami, went to the Charge Office and found a solitary constable in charge. On enquiring the whereabouts of the Member i/c, the officer was informed that he was '*lapa lo mugodi*'. The A/C finally took the officer to a corner of the camp where Lofty was sitting by a large hole from which bandits were carrying baskets of mica. Two more bandits sat clipping 'books'.

'What is the meaning of this, Corporal Lloyd?' demanded the officer. 'Why sir, the old rubbish pit was getting full up, so we are just digging another,' came the reply. And Corporal Lloyd was posted shortly afterwards. I don't know whether the story is true or not, but you must admit, it's a good 'un.

And if it isn't true, how did the clippings get there? because there they were ~ and I've seen them.

STARS IN HIS EYES

Once upon a time, the present Bishop of Matabeleland told me (when he was Rector of Marandellas where I was stationed) that one of the things which had triggered off his latent vocation to the ministry was seeing a film in which Spencer Tracey or Bing Crosby played a priest, and him (the Bishop, that is) thinking how well he would look in a cassock. Looking back, I well recall a film which had a rather different effect on my life. The film was *Green for Danger*, one of the old Pinewood Studio productions. They don't make films like that any more. It was a murder yarn, set in a hospital, and the investigating officer was that incomparable comedian, Alistair Sim. He hammed it up a bit, I think ~ for instance, as he walked up to the hospital, he heard the sound of a buzz-bomb (what V-1s used to be called), and dived over a dry stone wall to take cover in a ditch. The sound grew louder, and Alistair Sim peeped over the top of the wall to see a badly-silenced motor-bike go past. But of course, he got his man (or was it his woman?) in the end, after making one or two bloomers. I remember him sitting on one of those revolving stools they have in operating theatres, hugging himself with glee, when he thought he'd solved the case. Just after that, someone else got killed, so he obviously hadn't. The point about all this is that after seeing that film, I became imbued with the ambition to become a detective. I wanted to wear a black felt hat, and carry a black briefcase, just like Alistair Sim, and solve murders with the same whimsical nonchalance.

In the fullness of time, I joined the Corps, and after a spell in Town, and a spell in District, I applied for and was received into the Department ... Baker Avenue, upstairs, end office on the left, Harold Thacker's section. After I had been received by the D.C.I.O., the late Slash Barfoot, subsequently Commissioner of Police, I walked into the office, and met Mr Thacker, Detective Sergeant John Reid and Detective George Gibbons. George had just completed his probation and, when I first saw him, he was preparing a docket for court. He had a half-ring binder, and was placing the documents ~ all of which he had carefully re-typed ~ into it. He had a ruler, and was making a faint pencil mark on the centre of the left hand margin of each document, punching it, affixing linen reinforcing rings to each hole, and reverently placing the document in the binder. My first reaction to this sight was, frankly, one of concealed scorn, because, I supposed in my innocence, George was whitening his marbles. I learned otherwise soon! The scale of equipment in those days was somewhat meagre. There was only one typewriter in the office. Johnny Reid was a busy (and, I think, very efficient) detective, and he used the machine a lot. Mr Thacker had his own portable but that, of course, was not for use by the likes of me. Thus, if I wanted to do any typing, I had to wait until John had finished and look pretty slippy doing whatever it was I had to do. My typing was of a fairly average standard; in fact, I thought then, and I still think, it was above average because due to a Demob course which I had managed to wangle before leaving the Army, I used all four fingers on both hands. However, the practice of over-typing an error was pretty general in the places I had been, and I accordingly did it in the Department. The first report I typed for Harold Thacker came back with a blue pencil scrawl across it: 'Get a rubber ~ and use it!'

After a fortnight in the section, I went out and bought a portable typewriter ~ the first of a series of machines of which the model on which I am typing these words is the latest. And, by golly, I got plenty of practice! On one occasion, I was given a routine enquiry from another government department which entailed looking up a record and typing half a page ~ no, three lines ~ of information. I took three drafts of that wretched letter into the S.W.O. before he would take it into the D.C.I.O. for his signature! And I had an eraser tied to the carriage, and I used it! I kept a copy of that letter on my file and used the identical layout for all subsequent letters. I was learning ~ though not what I had fondly imagined I was going to learn. I was learning that if anything at all went out from the Department, it was right. It was boasted ~ with justification, I believe ~ that if a docket was sent to the Public Prosecutor, he need not even look at it before he got into court; all he had to do was to open it at Statement 1, call the name of the witness, lead the evidence, sit down, and call for the name of the witness on the second statement after cross-examination.

Mind you, such a reputation was not gained without some

effort. On one occasion, the D.C.I.O. was administering a rebuke. (Looking back, this seemed to occur quite frequently.) As his peroration, he said, 'Do you think you are busy, Fall?' 'Well, sir,' I replied, modestly, 'I think I shift a fair amount of work.'

'It has been noticed that you leave the office most evenings at five-thirty,' said the D.C.I.O. 'If you can get away at that time every evening, you can't be very busy.' That remark impressed itself on my mind ~ though not, perhaps, in quite the way in which Mr Barfoot had intended.

Some time later I was put in charge of a section ~ the Cycle Theft Section! In those days, anything from five to ten bicycles were reported stolen in the Salisbury area every day and as each report was received, two cards ~ a pink one and a yellow one ~ had to be typed and filed. One was filed in the makers' number order, the other in the Municipal registration number order, so that a suspected recovered cycle could be checked very quickly. Occasionally the entire section (consisting of myself and three African Detectives) would take this wretched file, set up a road-block with the aid of a couple of African details from the local section, and painstakingly check the numbers of all cycles passing the road-block. I loathed this stunt quite whole-heartedly. Apart from the fact that one seldom picked up a stolen bike this way (most were reports that had not been cancelled on recovery of the bike by the owner), it was very far indeed from my imagined detective procedure. Can you imagine Alistair Sim checking bikes at a road-block?

I remained in Mr Thacker's section whilst in charge of cycles, and every so often we were Duty Section. This entailed manning the office during the hours of darkness. The junior-but-one detail came on in the afternoon at four and worked until midnight, and the very junior detail came on at ten and worked until six the next morning. So, from midnight until six in the morning, the illustrious Salisbury C.I.D. was represented by one miserable Probationer Detective! And very miserable he would be as he struggled to stay awake. Frequently, I would find myself practically asleep over my desk at three or four in the morning, and would sally out into the night, to walk down to the end of Manica Road and back, just to keep myself awake. The pie-carts still stood in Railway Avenue and I usually went there for my midnight meal. Not that the curry and rice on offer was particularly digestible but it was a good deal more palatable than bacon and eggs dished up in the little dining room on the back stoep of the Baker Avenue station. One night, a report was received from Marlborough (which in those days came under the Avondale Police) that an African had broken into a house, assaulted the elderly female occupant before absconding, but had been fired at by the son of the elderly female aforesaid. I went out there to find Inspector Joe Starling on the scene, together with a couple of Avondale details. The assault was a relatively minor one, involving a blow on the head with a knife when the elderly lady had been awakened and screamed.

The firing had been done with a .22 pistol properly owned by the lady's son. The absconding housebreaker had not stolen anything, had not been hit by the bullets, and had not left any identifiable tracks. Joe Starling had dutifully instructed a couple of Avondale constables to carry out patrols in the area until dawn and there didn't seem much more that could usefully be done. I said as much to Joe Starling, he agreed, so we pushed off home. Naturally, I left a report before going off duty but did nothing else. At 8.00 a.m., or shortly thereafter, I was awakened by John Reid, with the news that the D.C.I.O. wanted to see me. I got dressed and cycled down to Baker Avenue. 'Why did you not call out the member-in-charge of your section?' 'Because it didn't seem to require that action, sir.' 'What made you think that?' 'Well, sir, I spoke to Inspector Starling, the Duty Inspector, and he agreed with me that everything that needed to be done had been done.' 'What had Inspector Starling to do with it?' 'Well, sir, he had already arrived on the scene, and naturally, I asked his advice.' 'Fall, when a member of the Department is called to the scene of a crime he takes charge, irrespective of the rank of any uniformed members who may be present.' (And if you don't believe that, that is true, ask any old hand who ever served in the C.I.D. The knife incidentally, was of the domestic variety which the intruder had picked up on site.)

Shortly after that, a report took me out on the Umtali road to a house at which another shooting incident had taken place. An African male had attempted to get into the house by the simple expedient of breaking out the glass from a French window. This had aroused the elderly occupants, the male member of which had come down to investigate. He brought with him an equally elderly .38 pistol. By the time that he reached the bottom of the stairs, the intruder had intruded. The occupant pulled the trigger and the revolver misfired. The intruder grappled, and they fell to the floor, struggling. This brought the elderly lady downstairs. She valiantly attempted to assist her husband by hitting the intruder over the head with a blunt instrument. Thus incensed, the intruder left the man and grappled with the woman, biting her in the side of the abdomen. The elderly gentleman recovered somewhat and went to the assistance of his wife. Between them, they managed to eject the intruder. Said ejection, however, did nothing to deter the criminal who promptly made an attempt to gain access through the window of a small office. The elderly gentleman, though considerably shaken, retrieved his revolver, removed the defective cartridge, and shot the intruder between the eyes ~ the intruder's head by this time being inside the window. When I arrived, I found the intruder lying on the ground outside the window, bleeding slightly and far from dead.

The ambulance arrived shortly after and the injured man was placed inside. It is worthy of note that as he was being placed in the ambulance, he sat up and roundly abused the attendants for their rough handling of him. (He died a couple of days later.)

After taking particulars, I returned to Baker Avenue and decided to advise my superiors. The senior members of my section were not available, the D.C.I.O. did not answer his phone, but ~ unluckily ~ the P.C.I.O. was in. So I told him. I say unluckily because, as you will have guessed, at eight the following morning I was hoicked out of bed to be told that notifying the P.C.I.O. of a case of this nature was not necessary. On the other hand, if the P.C.I.O. had not answered his phone, who knows ... I might have given the Commissioner of Police a bell. Which would possibly have been even less necessary.

One of the most interesting cases in which I was involved whilst in the Department, and one which indirectly contributed to my conviction that my peculiar genius was not being used to best advantage in the C.I.D. was that of the man with the dog. One Sunday afternoon, a man with a dog approached two little girls, and asked them if they would like a canary. One said that she would and accompanied the man, with the dog, to a spot near where the Minister of Finance's house now stands (but which was then an overgrown plantation) where she was raped. When I came on duty at 4.00 p.m. (or was it 5.00 p.m. on Sundays?) I was told to assist another junior member of the Department in a house-to-house check to ascertain who had seen a man, a girl and a dog pass their house that afternoon. This was done. Some time later, suspicion centred on a youth from South Africa who had left Rhodesia the morning after the incident. In order to strengthen the case against him, the Alsatian dog which he had been leading was put on an identification parade with nine other dogs. Of nine witnesses, four identified the dog positively, and two tentatively. I have a photograph of the line-up because I was holding the suspect dog. The youth was subsequently collected from South Africa by Mr Thacker who was obliged to spend Christmas and New Year in Cape Town. However desirable that might have been to some members, Mr Thacker was a thoroughgoing family man and did not enjoy his enforced sojourn to the Cape at all.

Anyway, shortly after the house-to-house check had been carried out, I was again in the D.C.I.O.'s office, again to receive a bottle about something or other. 'And another thing, Fall,' said the D.C.I.O., 'I had a complaint about you from an influential member of the public the other day. You took part in a house-to-house check, didn't you?' I agreed that I had. 'Yes, well, this member of the public said that he didn't believe that you were a member of the C.I.D. He said that you had a far-away look in your eye. Other members of the Department have commented on that as well.' I was, so to speak, properly took aback. 'I'm sorry, sir, I don't think I've ever had that complaint made about me before. I don't quite know what to do about it.' 'Nor do I, but you'd better do something.' (I know who that 'influential member of the public' was, too. He was a member of the then Cabinet. Confound his impudence.)

But, as you may have gathered, the writing was on the wall for Fall, regardless of the impertinent comments from the Cabinet. The end came at Christmas. I had contracted to appear in an amateur theatrical performance (at which I rather fancied myself). It was for charity and it was taking place at Christmas. When the Christmas and New Year duties came out, I found that my duties conflicted with the dress rehearsal and one of the performances. I quickly went round to my mates and offered to do Christmas Eve and New Year's Eve if they would do the nights when my public needed me. Subject to the S.W.O.'s approval, they agreed (not surprisingly). I went and very humbly requested permission to make the swap. After a good deal of humming and hawing, the S.W.O. agreed to my making the exchange after I had pointed out that I was not getting out of anything. 'But', said the S.W.O, 'a member of the Department is not supposed to have any interests outside his work.'

I had nearly completed my probation but I went to the D.C.I.O. and suggested that perhaps my talents could more usefully be employed ~ not to say appreciated ~ in the District Branch. To this suggestion, he most cordially assented and, shortly thereafter, I found myself at Mount Darwin ~ a very much more peaceful spot then than it has since become. We parted without rancour, and though I have, perhaps, highlighted the more trying aspects of the period I spent in the Department, it was a very valuable part of my Police career. Apart from the improvement in my typing, the whole standard of my presentation went up, because you cannot work for a bunch like that without taking on some of their attitudes ~ and their attitude towards work and presentation was that the best will get by ~ but only just. And, what is more, they were a good bunch, so that even if their attitude towards their profession was rather more exacting than mine, they were right to adopt it.

But it all goes to prove one thing. It's all right for some people (like the Bishop of Matabeleland) to get their inspiration for a career from the cinema. Despite Alistair Sim's great example, it most certainly wasn't right for me.

REMEMBERING MEMBERS-in-CHARGE

Members-in-Charge all used to have their strongly marked idiosyncrasies. I don't mean to imply that they were queer, just that they seemed to have clearly defined individualities which impressed themselves upon my youthful susceptibility ~ probably because Members i/c with troops like me under their command felt that it was essential to make an impression, or allow the station to degenerate into chaos. I'll give you an instance (I'll give you several, in fact). My first district station's Member i/c was very musical. In fact, he could play the piano by ear (which, incidentally, does not mean that he did not use his fingers, but that he could play a tune after having heard it only once or twice). And yet, he had the most appalling and far from appealing fondness for a singer named Mario Lanza who was making the charts in those days and who sang a particularly revolting number called Be My Love. Every time this thing was played, the Member i/c would turn up the radio, and drool.

I remember one occasion with this same Member i/c when, having been on a day patrol (me, not him), the tyre on the motorbike punctured. Not having a puncture repair outfit with me, I hitched a lift back to camp and walked into the quarters rather than the office ~ it being after 4.30 p.m. I told the Member i/c what had happened, expecting to be told to take the station truck out to fetch the bike. No way! All the Member i/c said was: 'Well you know where the repair outfit is. Hitch a lift back and repair it.' Which I proceeded to do after an offended silence that seemed to affect the Member-in-Charge not at all. Quite remarkable!

In those days, Members i/c were usually distinguished by the possession of a motorcar ~ a distinction rarely enjoyed by their subordinates. I remember having to relieve at a two-man station whilst the regular Member i/c was studying for his 2/Sergeant to 1/Sergeant Examinations. I noticed there was a slight discrepancy in the vehicle log book and commented on it to the junior member of the section. 'Oh,' he replied, 'the Member i/c likes to keep a mileage reserve in hand. We always enter a few extra miles in the log.' It became apparent that the individual concerned did not possess a car, but did have a wife with whom he shared no aversion to accepting invitations to dinner from local residents. The mileage reserve he liked to keep in hand was to enable him to take the station truck out in the evening, without the tiresome necessity of thinking up an excuse for so doing. 'Public Relations' were not acceptable buzz words in those days.

Another Member i/c did have a car because I saw it, standing pristinely in a shed on the station. It had been driven there on this individual's arrival and never left it during his tenure of office. This worthy never bothered to falsify returns ~ he merely booked himself out on a 'road patrol' if he wanted to go any- where. I remember one occasion when I was going to the local club to rehearse a play. I asked if anyone wanted to accompany me but there were no takers. After the rehearsal ~ which was held on the Club Secretary's night off ~ the cast duly repaired to the pub for a drink. Who should be propping up the bar of the pub but the Member i/c. He had decided to do a late evening road patrol. On another occasion, this same Member i/c had ventured out one Saturday afternoon ~ on a road patrol, of course. He had not bothered to advise me of this fact ~ he seldom did. At about five-thirty, a couple of the lads from the

Native Department dropped by the camp and asked if I wanted to go with them to the pub. I agreed and off we set. At our destination we found ~ naturally ~ the Member i/c recovering from the labours of his road patrol. I was a little piqued the following morning when the Member i/c saw fit to tell me that he did not like the station left unattended and in future would I be good enough to refrain from leaving it in his absence!

I served on one town station where the Member i/c was a stickler for records. Each morning, he would come into the Charge Office, go to the Occurrence Book, read through the entries for the preceding twenty-four hours and note ~ in red ~ any omissions he detected. He would then go to the C.R. and repeat the process, then to the D.B., the P.P.B., the Lost and Found Property Books and so on, noting any discrepancies. It was the duty of the Charge Office Sergeants (of whom I was one) to examine the records when coming on shift, and rectify any errors or omissions. In retrospect, this fastidiousness was perfectly justified because that particular station allowed of no slackness. Any matter which was overlooked for twenty-four hours simply passed out of our ken. The volume of work was really quite considerable. However, this daily procedure never failed to tickle us and I could not refrain from enquiring one morning whether the Member i/c had spotted my deliberate mistake? He wasn't at all sure whether I meant it or not, so merely grunted, and retired into his office.

His successor was a health-food fanatic. I used to watch fascinated as my Member i/c consumed his lunch, brought to the station in a plastic bag. A hard-boiled egg, a large piece of cheese, two slices of whole-meal bread thickly spread with butter, a heart of lettuce, a tomato or two, and vegetables, as they say, in season, used to be ingested with enormous relish ~ and no salt whatever. I asked him how he could bear to eat his food without salt and he replied that he liked the flavour of boiled eggs better than the flavour of salt. My tentative opinion that salt enhanced the flavour of food was scornfully rebutted and all condiments were consigned to perdition.

The surprising thing about this gentleman is that although he was a nut about natural foods ~ or perhaps because of it ~ he was the very picture of blooming good health, the best advertisement for vegetarianism I have ever seen. A man of parts too, who taught me how to make whole-meal bread, and demonstrated just how good homemade beer and wines could be. In the days when many district stations had two or three European details on them ~ a 2/Sergeant, plus one or two Troopers, Members i/c were very vulnerable matrimonially. It was not only, I think, that they had cars (not all of them did) or that they were paid all that much more money (they weren't) but the Member i/c was a not inconsiderable figure in the district and, be his subordinates never so attractive, he carried the mantle of authority. I can think of two Members i/c who married just about the only marriageable females in their respective sections ~ not that I'm suggesting that they wouldn't have married them anyway, but there was little doubt that a 2/Sergeant in charge of a station was a very much more glamorous marriage prospect than a 2/Sergeant serving under, for instance, a C/Inspector.

One Member i/c under whom I served actually reached the rank of Sub/Inspector after about seventeen years of service and, in recognition of this achievement, purchased his first motor car ~ an enormous, and nearly vintage Chevrolet. He had five children, which accounted, in part, for the fact that he had never before owned a car. He decided to christen the car by going to Durban with the entire family. On the day before he was due to set off, he ran a big end, and sending down to the local garage for a spare, he whipped off the sump, and replaced it. When he got to Johannesburg, he ran four big ends ~ on a Saturday morning no less! Nothing daunted, he chatted up a garage proprietor who took the Member i/c, his family, his car and the necessary spares home with him, put up the family for the weekend and effected the repairs to the car in time to send them off on Monday morning. That Member-in-Charge's distinguishing characteristic was an absolutely irresistible, although somewhat bluff, charm.

My wife and I were stationed in that Member i/c's bailiwick at the time of our marriage (my fiancée was the District Nurse) and we picked up some of our furniture from Salisbury on the station truck that was making a convenient duty run into town. The Member i/c embarrassed my fiancée very considerably ~ despite her calling ~ by his loud and pointed comments on one article of furniture as it was being loaded onto the roof carrier of the Land Rover. It was the double bed! No one in Manica Road or at the hostelry at which we stopped to refresh ourselves on the way back to the station could have been in any doubt as to the destination and purpose of the load which was lashed onto the roof.

Stable Parade was always a revealing sort of time on district stations. Most Members i/c used to come to the office in tee shirt and jeans (as did the men) but one martinet I served under always paraded in full uniform, shaved and bathed. This behaviour we found extremely odd, since it must have entailed rising at about 5.30 a.m., if not earlier.

Most Members i/c were somewhat less than meticulous about the ration issue, leaving that chore to the African N.C.O. or possibly the senior trooper. But again, one Member i/c of my acquaintance invariably issued the provisions himself with the Ration Roll in front of him and actually marked the amounts he issued in the book at the time at which he issued them! Something to do with ensuring that the hand that feeds was secured from being bitten perhaps. Still, it is perhaps not surprising that that individual reached the rank of Senior Assistant Commissioner. (So, incidentally, did the individual who made the daily check of the O.B., C.R., etc. Attention to detail is not without its rewards!)

Members i/c varied in the degree of welcome they afforded their subordinates. On one occasion I recall arriving at the station and being treated to a very earnest harangue by the Member i/c during which he assured me that this was no longer a punishment station, and that he was sure that I would enjoy my stay there. I did, too, because it was the briefest posting of my police career. No sooner had I left his office than I was recalled and told that a message had been received from D.H.Q. directing that I be returned back to the station down the road. I didn't even sleep at the camp.

On the other hand, there was the Member i/c who was not around when a friend of mine pitched up to join the strength ~ his first posting out of Depot. He found a servant who indicated a vacant room into which my friend pitched his kit. After a while a bell rang and my friend went out onto the stoep where the table was laid for supper. The other trooper emerged from his room reading a book, glanced at my friend, said good evening, sat down and went on reading his book. The Member i/c came out of his room, also reading a book, greeted my friend briefly, sat down, and went on reading his book. The newcomer struggled to make some sort of conversation but only managed to extract monosyllabic answers from his two companions. I was not present at that meal, but I was present at a meal with the same Member i/c at which the only conversation went like this.

'Are there any mashed potatoes?' 'No,' I replied. 'I don't care for vegetables with fish.' (I was mess caterer and had provided haddock and poached eggs.) 'Oh, well, next time, get the cook to make some for me, will you?' 'Certainly.' And not another word was spoken. Funnily enough, I only ever served on one station at which I could not get on with the Member i/c. This can't have been his fault entirely because other men managed to serve with him quite happily. And it can't have been entirely my fault either, because I managed to rub along with other Members i/c! Just put it down to a conflict of personalities. We shared one thing in common which was a degree of proficiency on the range and a fondness for musketry exercise. In fact, we both managed to shoot for the Force ~ in very much reserve positions. This didn't provide the occasion for disagreement, though I think it is true to say that when we shot on the same range, our first concern was to beat the other. We were evenly matched, too, and sometimes he beat me, and sometimes I beat him. Anyway, the O.C. was doing a visit, or short report or something, and asked me whether I wanted to speak to him about anything. I said that I did. The O.C. asked me whether I wanted the Member i/c to leave the room and I said I didn't much mind since what I had to say concerned the Member i/c. When I had explained that I felt that we were not a very well assorted team, the O.C. dryly remarked that he had been aware of an atmosphere from the moment that he arrived at the camp! Several weeks later, I was posted ~ the only occasion on which I ever asked for a transfer.

Members i/c had their crosses to bear too (as I later found out). On at least two occasions my Member i/c was directed to go and apologise to irate members of the public who had taken exception to something that I had said and had put the squeak in to the O.C. District ~ or possibly had gone higher than the O.C. because, generally speaking, I don't think that District O.C.s were all that susceptible to complaints of that nature.

Yes, Members i/c had their funny little ways ~ but they also had the best appointment going. When my half-section was contemplating retirement, which was after several years in commissioned rank, I asked him why he wanted to go. There were several reasons, but the one he confessed to being most heartfelt was that never again could he be in charge of a station. A District probably, even a Province perhaps, but not a station.

I think I know what he meant.

HORSE PATROLS

It was some time before I rode again after leaving Depot but then I was sent to Banket. RH *Junior* was the station's horse. A good steady nag he was ~ had he been any steadier he would have been motionless. But he would walk on all day if he had to.

One time, just after Christmas, a miner up on the Dyke came off shift, had a few refreshing jars at the Beerhall, went to his quarters and found that his wife had omitted to prepare his scoff. In a fit of pique, he dinged her with his mine lamp. Unfortunately, he hit her too hard and she died. The miner took off for the hills.

The Member-in-Charge, seeing a chance of whacking up some patrol mileage for *Junior*, sent me mounted minewards to track down the murderer. John Restorick, who had recently joined Laurie Davenport on Dog Section, arrived with a couple of hounds which would be put on the trail if and when I encountered it. After a week during which we had smelled nothing of the wanted man, much less seen him, John was fed up and announced that he was taking his dogs home. The next day I burst a girth so, after patching it up with a piece of reim, set off to follow him back to camp. Thirty five miles it was, near enough, and having left at 5.30 a.m., it was 4.30 p.m. when we reached the station. By the time we got back, both *Junior* and I had totally lost interest in the whole proceedings. The day after, while we were still thinking about what to do next, a couple of the mine's police boys came into camp with the murderer. He had tired of swanning around the hills and had given himself up to them.

Another time we got word at Banket that one of the Depot's remount laddies wanted the taste of rural patrol so the Member-in-Charge told me to meet up with the volunteer at Trelawney and take him up the Dyke. I can't recall the name of the remount man but I can remember the horse; RH *Legal* ~ a great wall-eyed Roman-nosed splay-footed idiot of an animal. Inspector Stephens, at that time Depot's chief equitation instructor, despatched the pair at 5.30 a.m. in full marching order and *Legal* reached Darwendale, some 40 miles away, at 8.30 p.m., having been led most of the way by his rider who had been shedding bits and pieces of equipment to passing motorists to lighten the load. That first day should have sent a message to me but I put it down to idle riding.

Anyway, at about 10.30 the following morning *Legal* and his rider bucketed up to Trelawney, we joined up and set off up the Dyke. As I've said, *Junior* could walk on all day but I got a bit acid with my companion because *Legal* just would not walk on. I was forced to keep reining *Junior* in ~ which he didn't like nor did it amuse me. After a couple of days of this, I told the other man to go on ahead. But it was obvious, even to me, that *Legal* was going dead lame on both hind feet. The animal had very tender heels but the farriers had never bothered to shoe him astern. The road up the Dyke was made up of spoil from the adits and was naturally pretty hard on the horses' feet. Finally I sent *Legal* back to Banket and finished the patrol by myself. By the time *Junior* and I got back to camp a week later, the remount rider had gone home by R.M.S. leaving *Legal* to rest his poor feet and eat his head off.

About a fortnight later, after *Legal* had enjoyed a nice rest, the Member-in-Charge told me to take him out for some exercise. It was a Thursday, the day driving tests were scheduled. Me, being a conscientious youth, would sometimes fail the more obviously incompetent applicants which caused the Member-in-Charge no little embarrassment. Sending me off with *Legal* meant he would be spared the necessity of explaining to irate members of the local aristocracy exactly why their wives/ daughters/tractor drivers had been denied the privilege of terrorising the rest of our population.

Anyway, off I went to give *Legal* a bit of a run around ~ only to discover very quickly that it was yours truly who was in for some violent exercise. The rest of that afternoon is a blank. I surfaced on the stoep, sipping very sweet tea with the ambulance driver from Sinoia. To put it mildly, I was concussed but ~ in my coma ~ I had brought *Legal* home, stabled him and returned the saddlery to the tack room and staggered into the Charge Office. It was there that my manner was recognised as being more than usually distrait, leading to the suspicion that something ~ probably me ~ had gone adrift. Inspection of *Legal*'s nose confirmed that we had both gone down while the G.M.O. reckoned that I had been biffed on the bonce and should be taken to hospital. Which was done and I had a very pleasant spell in hospital. The Sinoia lads used to visit most evenings to help me lower the level of the bottle of Johnny Walker in my locker and the nurses as always, were kindness itself. By the time I got back to Banket, *Legal* had been walked back to Depot by an African Constable.

The last horse patrol I did was at Goromonzi. We didn't have a horse at Goromonzi but two remount riders brought out three nags and I was told to take our visitors out for a run round the section. I should have known better and gone sick but some people only learn the hard way. Off we went and by the end of the first day I had lamed my horse.

As my senior readers will know, this was a crime compared to which arson, rape or murder were but mere peccadilloes. The O.C. nearly did his nut, that worthy being Lt. Col. Fitzwilliam, so, again, my older readers can readily imagine the fulminations which must have struck Robert John, my Member-in-Charge, when my mortal sin was reported. 'T-t-t-tell F-f-f-fall to f-f-f-finish the patrol on a pp-push b-b-bike,' was the gist of the command from on high. (Fitz had a speech impediment which was particularly evident when he was upset.)

I was issued with the station pushbike and returned to the base camp. Goromonzi, as Salisbury District veterans will know, had a large farming area and it was the farms we had been instructed to visit. Each morning one or other of the two remount riders (Rowe and Rowland, if my memory serves me) would sally forth. The horse, being fresh, would gallop off towards the horizon while the constable and I cycled along in its wake. We would meet up at the farm turnoff, approach the farmhouse and get the patrol visit sheet signed before taking our leave. By this time, however, the Depot nag would no longer be in the mood to gallop. After all, it was accustomed to doing the early morning ride, then eating its fat head off in the paddock all day.

Now a walking horse proceeds at about four and a half miles per hour ~ a fast pace for a walker. But a bicycle is difficult to ride at such a slow pace, particularly in sand. Even a trot at between six and eight miles an hour is too slow to cycle comfortably alongside. So now the two cyclists would proceed to the next farm turnoff, fall out, have a smoke and wait for the bold equestrian to pitch up. Then would come the slow advance to the farmhouse to the admiring glances of the farmer and/or his wife and suggested intimidation of the local lay-abouts, the ceremonial signing of the patrol sheet and on again.

Very galling it was for me, I can tell you. Rowe or Rowland mounted on their magnificent steeds while I was perched astride the menial velocipede. All in all, exactly the kind of humiliation Fitz had in mind.

By early afternoon, the horse was a definite brake on the progress of the patrol so I would send the mount and its rider back to camp while the African constable and I knocked off a couple more farms. I was out daily but the two Depot lads lazed about on alternate days. Ever since that memorable patrol, I have been willing to challenge any horseman to race me over any distance beyond fifty miles with what he can carry on his horse and what I can carry on my bicycle. My challenge has never been taken up but it is now too late ~ advancing years have made me less of a cyclist than I was then.

Next time I was in D.H.Q., the District Clerk told me that the O.C. wanted to see me ~ a contingency I had rather anticipated. For ten minutes solid, Fitz called me every kind of adjectival fool he could lay tongue to ~ coping remarkably well, I thought, with his speech impediment. Then he told me that he knew that I was about to be promoted to Sergeant and that he had not wanted to blast my career by charging me with negligence for laming the horse. And that is one reason ~ there are others ~ why I am convinced that Fitz was the best officer I ever served under, notwithstanding the fact that there were other pretty good ones.

RH *Junior* has been in horse heaven these many years. I heard that he gave as little trouble in his dying as he had in his living. One morning, when the detail went in to turn him out for stable parade, there he was ~ dead. I have a shoe which the farrier made for him on one of his periodic visits but never fitted. Carted it around in my kit ever since I left Banket and now it hangs on the wall of my little study with my spurs tastefully arranged around it. Looks attractive as a wall decoration ~ sort of *objet trouve*. And there the shoe and my spurs will continue to hang because if they do form a mounted infantry section, I'll be there ~ but not on a horse.

This Obituary for John Fall appeared in the U.K.
Outpost Autumn, 2002

4479/5420 John David McPherson 'Gus' Fall passed away on 7 August 2002, aged 73 years, having collapsed while giving a sermon on the previous Sunday. 'Gus' served from 18 October 1949 to 11 December 1955, as 4479, and again as 5420 from 9 June 1956 to 31 January 1962, when he took his discharge as a Sergeant.

Having left the B.S.A. Police 'Gus' took the cloth and became Chaplain to the Rhodesian Army.

When he returned to England he suffered a heart attack and took early retirement, settling in West Mersey. Never one to be idle 'Gus' undertook services in the Colchester diocese and this was particularly pertinent for 'funerals', having been well schooled from his Army Chaplin days.

Gus is survived by his wife Alison, their son Alistair and daughter Gillian.

The Rev. 'Gus' Fall

1960s

BIG CHANGES in the NINETEEN-SIXTIES

John Berry 5584
Compiled from various sources, including *The Outpost*

During the 1960s some major changes occurred in the structures of the B.S.A. Police. This was due to a greater recognition of the role of the African Police and due to crime becoming more sophisticated and requiring more scientific methods to aid in investigating and preparing cases for Court.

Much greater demands were placed upon the Force due to the upsurge in urban violence. A number of specialised branches and sections were created to deal with specific areas in the field of maintaining law and order. The need to combat insurgency later in the decade led to the formation of the Police Anti-Terrorist Unit (P.A.T.U.), which was greatly expanded in the 1970s.

General Packard's Report of 1962 subsequently led to changes in the rank structure, and the rank of Constable (European) was now Patrol Officer, while the rank of Sergeant was now Section Officer. The word African was dropped and the African Constable and Sergeant became Constable and Sergeant. Other changes saw the formal establishment of a Special Branch and reorganisation of Districts and Provinces, and later the establishment of an independent intelligence-gathering body, the C.I.O. (Central Intelligence Organisation), which, however, was staffed by former members of the B.S.A. Police.

The Specialist Sections formed or expanded were numerous and this short article covers only a few. Sometime in the future, no doubt, a comprehensive account of all such sections will be undertaken. Covered in this account are:

The Forensic Laboratory.

The Armaments and Bomb Disposal Section.

Development and Research into Mine-proofing Vehicles.
River Patrol.

Formation of Police Anti-Terrorist Unit (P.A.T.U.).

The Forensic Laboratory

In 1962, Dr John Thompson was appointed Forensic Scientist to the Force. He founded the Forensic Laboratory and much of the credit for the services it now provides was due to him. At the outset, Dr Thompson's prescription for Police/Scientist Liaison – now a cornerstone of the organisation – was introduced. Never remote to young Investigating Officers in need of guidance, he was always willing to interrupt his work to assist.

While policemen have a responsibility to keep themselves abreast of developments in forensic science, it is doubtful whether many of them realise how complete a revolution has taken place in chemical analysis over the last few decades. Prior to World War II, 'analysis' relied chiefly on traditional techniques which scarcely left the realm of litmus paper, filter paper and relatively unsophisticated items of laboratory glassware. Instrumentation technology has over-thrown the reign of beakers and test-tubes and 'black boxes' have caused tremendous strides in speed and accuracy and a much broader capability and increased sensitivity.

Evidence in the whole gamut of crimes – from murder, arson, rape, driving offences to poaching and bombings – is now analysed in the laboratory where the precision of machines is coupled with the essential human brainpower.

Gas Chromotography provides an invaluable instrument for analysing blood. The machine can analyse a pin-prick of blood and break it down into its constituents, for example alcohol content.

Infra-red Spectroscopy analyses various drugs, both narcotic and toxic, so that they may be identified. A suspect substance taken, for example, from the body of a deceased, can be positively identified by the infra-red analyser. Accuracy is essential so that a successful prosecution in Court can result.

The Electroporesis instrument is used for identifying species of blood – that is, whether a blood sample or smear taken from a scene or the belongings of an accused comes from a human or an animal – and, if the latter, what breed of animal it is. An instance of this was where an accused in Gwanda was cleared of stock theft charges when the blood stains on his clothes proved to be those of an impala and not a cow.

The Emission Spectograph Analyser is used to match up substances found at the scene with those found on or near the accused and matches up pieces of metal, glass, paint and even plants by their trace element composition. Cases have been referred to the Laboratory where it has had to be established whether mealies have come from one field or another. A small sample of the substance is vaporised in an electric arc and radiation readings of the spectrum will establish the trace element characteristics of the sample for cross matching.

The Armaments Section
In 1963, the Armaments Section, incorporating Ballistics and Bomb Disposal, became more formalised and expanded, with Staff Inspector Don Hollingworth in charge, assisted by Staff Sergeant Dave Perkins.

Many hundreds of thousands of fired cartridge cases were processed by the Ballistics team over the years and matched against outstanding scenes of crime. This involved the taking of many thousands of photomicrographs.

An example was in 1966 when an Indian couple were fired upon while travelling from Zambia to Salisbury. The vehicle was not hit but cartridge cases were left at the scene and recovered by D/Inspector John Fletcher. These cartridge cases were found to have identical firing markings to some found at the scene of the 'Battle of Sinoia' and so proved to be the same group of terrorists.

The Section (under overall direction of Sen. Asst. Comm. Guy Houghton) was also responsible for the research, development and ultimately life-saving design of the mine-protected Land Rover and later Rhino and other vehicles. The importance of these vehicles cannot be overstated as they allowed relatively safe movement of personnel in mined areas during the bush war of the 1970s.

A dramatic instance of Bomb Disposal work occurred in 1977 when Don Hollingworth defused a time bomb which had been deposited in the Railways Left Luggage Office, Salisbury. On the same day, a bomb (an improvised device incorporating a land-mine) exploded in Woolworths, Salisbury, killing eleven people and injuring seventy-seven.

The Boats Section
No doubt from very early days, *ad hoc* use was made of boats for emergency duties on the Zambesi River. Tpr. Jack Hoddinott wrote of his using a boat during a long patrol in 1928. In 1954 a launch was used to patrol the Zambesi between Kariba and Kanyemba (before Lake Kariba came into being). In 1964 a police launch, the *Sir John Chancellor*, was used for regular patrol and transport duties on the lake. Over time and to meet

its operational requirements, the section grew until in 1971 it had seven boats on strength. Repairs and maintenance of the boats were undertaken by private firms and this was found unsatisfactory. The B.S.A. Police Marine Workshops came into being in 1971, under Inspector Buddy Wilson, assisted by Jeff Howard. Thanks to the efforts of a lot of people (too many to be named) the section forged ahead in leaps and bounds. Funds were found to purchase tools, special equipment, new motors and hulls. In addition to the normal running repairs that make up more than an average day's work for the technicians, supply problems and an increase in the Force's river-patrol commitments prompted the section's involvement in the design and building of launches suitable for current Police operations, especially in the anti-terrorist role.

One of the major breakthroughs for the Section was the development of the jet boat, that is a hull propelled, not by the conventional propeller which can cause difficulties in very shallow water, but by a jet of water expelled by a sophisticated motorised pump. This type of craft had been tried and tested by private firms in Rhodesia without much success and was thought to be a waste of time. Messrs Wilson and Howard took over a rejected jet boat and turned it into a very successful police launch – which was, in fact, the predecessor of a further five police jet boats. It was the jet boat's development by the Section and the skilful handling by such district policemen as Tom Naude, Pete Standaloft, Julian Twine and other members, then stationed at Chirundu and Kanyemba, that managed to open up the Zambesi as far as river patrols and security work was concerned.

The jet boats patrolled the Zambesi from below Kariba Dam to Kanyemba on the Mozambique border – a distance of some 170 miles. A considerable distance to be covered and while the district policeman of today skims the sandbanks in 18 inches of water at 35 mph, he should think back on the old river hands who battled with leaky hulls and damaged propellers in carrying out patrols in very difficult conditions. In 1977 there were 20 police-owned launches.

The Field Reserve made a huge contribution in maintaining and repairing the boats and in the later stages provided a Police Reserve Marine Wing on Lake Kariba, manned by reservists using their own craft.

Nicknamed 'Jaws', this troop barge was badly damaged while in service with the South African Police and was rebuilt by the Police Marine Workshops and was used for carrying troops on Lake Kariba. A Field Reserve technician maintains a jet boat engine (right)

Formation of the Police Anti-Terrorist Unit (P.A.T.U.)

Terrorist attacks mounted by dissidents who had been trained outside Rhodesia and who infiltrated the country from the north intent on creating as much terror and dislocation of law and order as their modest numbers would allow, were already a problem in 1963. In the previous December a prominent nationalist had been found in possession of three smuggled sub-machine guns and two pistols. In July 1964 the infamous 'Crocodile Gang' murdered Mr Petrus Oberholzer near Melsetter and two months later a gang crossed at Victoria Falls to mount the unsuccessful attack on Dube Ranch on the Shashi.

The first large incursion came in April 1966 and on 17 May Mr and Mrs Johannes Viljoen were murdered at Nevada Farm, Hartley. A gang, similar to that responsible for the Viljoen murders and which was believed to have crossed into Rhodesia with those who attacked Nevada Farm, had been located on the outskirts of Sinoia at the end of April. A combined Police/ Army/Rhodesian Air Force exercise, 'Operation Pandora', in which Police regular force and reserve members of V.A.T. (Volunteers for Advanced Training) played a notable part, was successful in eliminating the terrorists. This particular incident, followed by 'Operation Nevada', served to underline the threat posed by increased numbers of the enemy.

Official reaction from Police Headquarters was not long in

130

coming. In mid-July 1966 a directive went out from P.G.H.Q. detailing the lessons learned at Sinoia and Hartley and followed by the instruction that basic anti-terrorist training for all regular policemen was to start immediately. Depending upon their showing during this basic training, volunteers would be selected for advanced anti-terrorist training.

In the meantime Chief Superintendent A.E.F. Bailey had been installed in P.G.H.Q. as Training Officer with a special responsibility for the new scheme. Two courses for Police anti-terrorist instructors had been held at the Gwelo School of Infantry and on 1 August 1966 the 'guinea-pigs' – Morris Depot's Recruit Squads 1 and 2/66 embarked on the first 'Police Anti-Terrorist Training Course.'

The first week of the course consisted of map reading, ground appreciation, theoretical rural operations, patrolling and weapon training. On 9 August the recruits and their instructors moved to the Horseshoe Block, east of the Sipolilo Farming Area, to carry out a variety of reconnaissance and training tasks. Some liaison was supplied during the exercise by the Police Reserve Air Wing. Among the many comments which resulted, these two are interesting:

'Although elephant were in the area, no interference with the patrol resulted,' and 'Three elderly Africans were found fishing in one of the rivers. They had been following this occupation since they were youngsters, but had never before seen Europeans in the area.'

So much for breaking new ground.

Chief Superintendent A.E.F. 'Bill' Bailey (left) is generally recognised as the founder of P.A.T.U. During WW II, he served with the Long Range Desert Group in North Africa and Southern Europe. Initially P.G.H.Q. was not keen on P.A.T.U., but tolerated Volunteers for Advanced Training (V.A.T.).
Inspector Reg Seekings (right) had served in the S.A.S. in North Africa in WW II where he had met C. Supt. Bailey.

Other lessons were learned. Ordinary issue boots were a perpetual source of trouble (and one which was not satisfactorily overcome for many years): the army's 24-hour ration packs were far too generous – and weighty – for practical purposes: only one-fifth of those taking part in the exercise, regardless of the fact that they were recruits in excellent physical condition, were assessed as being really suitable for the duties envisaged, and it was found that men in the older age group, perhaps paradoxically, were better able than their younger companions to withstand sustained periods of physical effort and discomfort. Another sardonic comment was:

> One of the hardest lessons to drum home to all is the need for perpetual observation and alertness and the necessity for silence at all times. The average man appears to find life without conversation difficult!

In the following months the growing pains of P.A.T.U. which had been inflicted on Recruit Squads 1 and 2/66 were felt by policemen all over Rhodesia. Bill Bailey and Reg Seekings toured the country explaining their objective, running training courses, assessing the response to their pleas and reporting back to P.G.H.Q. By the end of November formal courses had taken place in all the Provinces, more Depot recruits had undergone training and basic anti-terrorist training had become part of promotion courses. Police reservists had similarly been drawn into the Bailey/Seekings net and the term 'P.A.T.U.' was already in common use.

Very soon it was realised that the units would benefit considerably by the inclusion of sergeants and constables who would act as interpreters. Selection of these members began with special attention being paid to those who had previously attended Outward Bound courses at Melsetter where physical endurance and bushcraft were important aspects of the leadership training syllabus.

Before Chief Superintendent Bailey left the Force at the end of November 1966, he chaired a committee consisting of Chief Superintendent Ted Sheriff (the then Staff Officer Planning), Chief Superintendent Harry Mason (Staff Officer Auxiliary and Security) and Superintendent Buck Buchanan, Bill Bailey's successor as Staff Officer (Training) with the special responsibility for the development of anti-terrorist training. As Provincial Superintendent (A&S) down at Salisbury Province,

Superintendent Ron Gardner and his 2 i/c, Inspector Derek Humberstone, were to play an important part in putting into practice the P.A.T.U. training policy emanating from P.G.H.Q.

By the end of January 1967 basic training had been completed and the formation of sections was well underway. At this stage the listed objectives of P.A.T.U. patrolling were to contact and arrest terrorists, pursuit and reconnaissance, ambush and observation.

The dedication of P.A.T.U. members themselves has been backed by tremendous support from the 'front office' and the 'backroom boys' over the years. The Quartermaster's concern that P.A.T.U. should be properly equipped had shown no sign of diminishing since Assistant Commissioner Phil Owen fought his battles on P.A.T.U.'s behalf in 1966. Although some argument still lingers over the respective merits of hockey boots and the sturdier but heavier issue footwear, P.A.T.U. members seem to have found their feet. The other battle for the issue of camouflage clothing to replace the old riot blues was eventually won. Another argument almost forgotten revolved over the choice of weaponry, the issue of grenades and the very basic problem of the quantity of equipment P.A.T.U. members *should* carry and the weight of supplies they *could* in practice carry without defeating the object of an extended patrol. And then there was the vote of thanks to the Finance Section who turned out *en mass* to ensure that every man involved in a particularly large operation received his allowances as he disembarked from vehicles at the Hard Square.

In one respect however the wheel of progress has turned full circle since the heady days of the V.A.T.s. With the regular police's ever increasing commitment to less exotic police duties, the P.A.T.U. role has largely been thrust upon the dedicated reservists of town and country. Their devotion, not only to operational duties but to the time-consuming demands of regular training, has been a singular example to some of the regular members who view their P.A.T.U. involvement with rather less enthusiasm.

Ready for deployment

Still in riot blues issue uniform

Return to base by helicopter

Half and half uniform

Base

P.A.T.U. teams

134

.... P. A. T. U.

.... the 'urban' farm patrolmen

Break for refreshment

African Police Reserve from various Provinces on training course

Airforce Provost at Centenary

Tracker Dog

Part of P.A.T.U. stick

Police Reserve Air Wing (P.R.A.W.) Photo: Courtesy Wayne Kennerly

P.A.T.U. Training with live ammunition

P.A.T.U. Training

1970s

AN INNOCENT AT THE SHARP END

Alan Stock
6063 British South Africa Police

NORTHERN MASHONALAND, February, 1973 – an area which, in its vastness, swallows up murder, wholesale subversion, gnawing uncertainty and, for the policeman sweating there, long days of sticky, unrelenting toil at what they call 'the sharp end'. To those of us at the other end, excluded from the drama, the region has an aura of nineteenth century 'Darkest Africa' and it is hard to conceal a frustration prompted by our ignorance of what is going on at Centenary and at the other small towns which have become ringed on so many maps. Perhaps this article, written by someone at the blunt end, will go some way towards alleviating the frustration if read in the context of the ordinary policeman's awareness of the overall security situation. Before I drove northward, I had no more idea than the majority of readers of the realities of the sharp end, so we all start from scratch.

It has been said too frequently over the last few years that Rhodesia is fighting a war. Some people believe that 'wolf' has been cried too often – with some justification when one considers the variety of definitions which might be accorded to 'war'. Military text-books will define for the purist just how many armed attacks have to be mounted, the precise nature and strength of the opposing forces, the degree of sophistication of the weapons being used and the host of other details which must be assessed and evaluated before a technically accurate announcement of war can be made. But only heads buried deep in the Mashonaland sandveld would argue the point in the current situation.

Having received official approval to prepare some sort of informative, illustrated article for publication in *Outpost*, one problem immediately arose. I was requested to put forward an itinerary for my proposed visit to the sharp end. In ignorance of the actual situation, the only counter was to suggest that I be allowed to place myself in the hands of the police officer on the combined security forces operational headquarters at Centenary. This was accepted and it is only fair to state that this article could not have been written without the full cooperation of this field headquarters.

Centenary is less than two hours drive from Salisbury, sobering factor number one to those who chose to ignore the seriousness of the situation. On the journey I tried to recall the sequence of attacks as relayed to the general public. These facts are worth consolidating here if only to present the picture as seen by the man in the street.

Just before Christmas, it was announced that terrorists had attacked Altena Farm, Centenary, on December 21 and that Jane, the eight-year-old daughter of farm owner Marc de Borchgrave, had received minor injuries. Mvuradona Store, north of Altena, was also attacked. A landmine was discovered on a nearby road.

Two days later Whistlefield Farm, Centenary, was attacked and Mr de Borchgrave and his nine-year-old daughter Ann, who were staying at Whistlefield after the Altena attack, received shrapnel wounds. A landmine blew up an army vehicle near Whistlefield and Corporal Norman Moore died later of his injuries. On January 3, another landmine exploded in a tribal trust land injuring D/P/O David Hawkes and two African soldiers.

On January 8, Constables Siegfried Marx and Owen Durham of the S.A.P. were killed in a landmine explosion near Victoria Falls. Injured were S/O Surkont, Sgt Mushipe and Constable Chirwodza of the B.S.A.P. Support Unit. Mount Darwin was unsuccessfully attacked resulting in superficial damage to the District Commissioner's office and to a road bridge south of the town.

Within the next three days two Lands Inspectorate officers, Messrs Robert Bland and Denis Sanderson, had been murdered in the Mount Darwin area and a third man, Mr Gerald Hawkesworth, was missing. Later reports from Africans who were with Mr Hawkesworth confirmed that he had been kidnapped by the terrorists.

On January 24, Ellan Vanin Farm was attacked and Mrs Ida Kleynhans died from injuries received when a grenade was thrown into her bedroom. Her husband, Chris, was wounded and the farm-house extensively damaged. On February 4, Chaona Farm was attacked, an elderly British visitor, Mr Leslie

Jellicoe, who was alone on his son's farm, was killed and several of the farm's buildings were fired as were a large number of African huts in the compound.

On February 21, on Charmwood Farm, Centenary, Mr Hannes Boshoff was subjected to an unsuccessful grenade attack by a lone terrorist – who killed himself with his second bomb. His death brought the tally of terrorist dead to approximately thirty with a larger number captured by Security Forces.

In normal times one might easily blink while driving north and miss Centenary completely. It's not quite so easy today. The conglomeration of Security Force tents, vehicles and radio aerials cannot be conveniently hidden.

Reporters are, by repute, hard cases, but I make no claim to such professionalism. Even a police uniform can't hide a degree of self-consciousness when one's brief is to pry into the affairs of those who have much more important things on their plates than to answer the naïve questions of the outsider. In such an atmosphere, perhaps I was the only one to detect a note of resignation in the greeting I received as I obeyed the large notice at the entrance to Centenary Police Station and reported my arrival to Control.

My first consideration was to absorb as much of the background and current information on the war situation as possible – and I was given every opportunity to do so, thanks to the police officers commanding Special Branch and C.I.D. detachments and the Border Control Officer, Mashonaland Province. The picture I drew was the result of their briefings then and personal experiences in the next few days. There is obviously a limit to what can be related here and it is worth emphasising that the following is a personal sketch of events, only vetted by official sources.

The facts of extra-territorial military training of would-be terrorists are no longer secret, neither are the locations of the training camps. But in recent times formal tuition in the waging of guerilla warfare has been amplified by real experience gained in other theatres of revolutionary operations and during this practical apprenticeship emphasis has been placed in obtaining the support of tribesmen in the 'war zones', this support being won either by fear or favour. Chairman Mao's advice to 'fishes in the ocean' and other equally rudimentary rules for revolutionaries are required reading for terrorists, not only those ranged against Southern Africa.

In the latter half of 1972 small gangs of hardcore, externally trained terrorists infiltrated the remote, desolate northern border areas and beyond with the intention of subverting the local population. Our north-eastern border is largely a matter of academic geography, there is no natural barrier such as the Zambesi to the west. However the region is still part of the Zambesi Valley – hot, wild and sparsely populated. It is virtually impossible to patrol the area effectively and the locals have scant regard for a line on a map, the significance of which escapes them. Generally, the inhabitants of the area are among the most primitive of Rhodesia's people.

The terrorist recruiting campaign in this part of the Zambesi Valley met with some success. The strategy used was intelligent, ruthless and efficiently carried out.

The tribesmen in the region are extremely superstitious and are particularly susceptible to the influence of the spirit mediums and witchdoctors of the area. This weakness was capitalised upon by the terrorists to the point of kidnapping one prominent female spirit medium who had a 'half-section' practising in the Sipolilo area. The interaction of these two halves of an ancestral deity was used extensively by the enemy to exact obedience. Other terrorist reconnaissance and recruiting groups brought with them into Rhodesia their own 'mystic figures', their shrouds of witchcraft concealing very active political ideologies. This use of primitive superstition by the terrorist organisation is worthy of a complete article on its own – but it requires much more than a three-day field trip to unravel.

There were other less mysterious methods of recruitment. Airy promises of good food, generous pay, the issue of sophisticated weapons and the obvious lure of a life of luxury 'after the struggle' persuaded some locals to join the enemy. And if a combination of spiritual blackmail and carrots failed to do the trick, there were the outright physical threats. Unsympathetic tribesmen, having been indicated as such by their fellows for the sake of a small reward or promise thereof, were forcibly abducted to terrorist bases in Mozambique and tortured as an example to others.

This type of penetration spread insidiously from the border areas. It may be over-simplifying things to say that where the bribery and blackmail of the primitive areas left off, the political sympathies of Africans in the more civilised reserves and tribal trust lands were cultivated to the maximum by the terrorist organisation. Former hotbeds of African nationalism were fired again, quietly and methodically, and the cancer of subversion spread up and over the Zambesi Escarpment.

The new recruits joined the hardcore terrorists in a variety of capacities. Some became militant arms-bearing terrorists themselves, having undergone crash courses of training. Others became porters for the large quantities of modern arms and ammunition that were brought into the country and hidden. Indications of some of the loads carried by these gangs over very rough country are almost unbelievable. Older tribesmen and women were enlisted to supply food and other comforts to the hardcore infiltrators, the local amateurs and their porters.

This then was how the stage was set towards the end of last year – not a pretty picture and one that was to get a lot worse before it improved.

On the morning of my arrival at Centenary a briefing session was held for section leaders of the local police reserve and members of the rural civil defence committee. It was a lengthy meeting and covered most of the ground recorded above. The army commander pulled no punches as he summed up after the Special Branch officer and army intelligence had interpreted the situation. The briefing was particularly valuable as far as I was concerned as it consolidated much of what I had already been told. Later the Staff Officer (Auxiliary Services) and the Superintendent (A.S.) Mashonaland Province, addressed the police reservists.

At lunchtime I found myself alongside the *Queen Mary* and no report of this nature would be complete without a tribute to the police reservists who run the mobile canteens. There is no glamour in sweating all day over a hot stove – ask any housewife – but at Centenary the crew of the *Queen Mary* have a hotter and longer day than anyone. Their customers, a large contingent of Air Force personnel as well as policemen, were predictably scathing about the similarity between tea, coffee and gravy served by the canteen, and the repetitive daily lunch menu of cold meats and salad came in for some good-humoured criticism. The catering staff gave as good as they got in the way of insults but beneath all the ribaldry was a deep appreciation of the function being performed so ably by the *Queen Mary* crew.

That afternoon I jumped at the opportunity of making myself useful! The C.I.D. team preparing the murder docket on the Chaona Farm attack were trying to find a way around the hours of draughtsmanship in preparing a plan of the farm. It was suggested that aerial views of the farm would satisfy the requirements of court.

Would I use my camera to some purpose?

We flew the few kilometres to Chaona Farm in an aircraft belonging to a member of the Matabeleland Police Reserve Air Wing after some ten minutes on the ground spent cleaning the perspex windows as carefully as possible. Taking photographs through perspex is an unpredictable business.

Chaona is on the southern edge of the Centenary farming area. Beyond and above the farm tower the rugged intimidating hills which form an almost impenetrable wall along the northern boundary of the Chiweshe Reserve. These gomos, in the appropriated vernacular of troops stationed in the area, are one of the main curses of anti-terrorist operations. A heart-breaking, energy-sapping combination of dense vegetation and sheer rock faces, the hills are riddled with caves and gullies, virtually ideal country for guerilla operations.

As we circled the farm, our pilot keeping a wary eye on the mass of rocks to the south, it was not difficult to reconstruct the ease with which the attack had been mounted and the long start a determined terrorist gang would have had at night before their tracks could be pursued in such country. Trying to follow the spoor of innocent wanderers over the rocky outcrops would have taxed the abilities of the best trackers; pursuing an enemy well versed in covering and confusing his tracks would be an almost impossible job.

On the other side of the farm were the access roads, vivid brown scars on the green countryside and obvious targets for the terrorist's latest weapon, landmines. Try to visualise the security forces team on their way to Chaona Farm on the night of February 4, anxious to get to the scene as fast as humanly possible. But how far from their objective must they slow down and begin the nerve-wracking, time-consuming search for mines ... two kilometres, three? Exactly how far away is the farm anyway? Perhaps this time the terrorists will try a new tactic – laying not only mines but an ambush on the road. And in the distance is the glow of burning huts, a winking invitation to cast discretion to the winds and blunder blindly on. If there is a theoretical solution to this kind of threat, who will put it to the test? This is the razor's edge of the sharp end.

A mention of mines bring to mind (pun intended) the tale of

the C.I.D. superintendent who was travelling to the scene in the same vehicle as the army engineers. In the darkness he got out of the truck when the convoy stopped and received detailed instructions from the army officer in charge regarding the 'path of exploration' required before the convoy could proceed. It was some time before the C.I.D. officer realised that he was being mistaken for the mine-clearing 'brown job' and that the investigation required by the army commander was hardly up his street.

The aerial photographic mission did not take long and we returned to Centenary where a degree of morbid anticipation was discernible. A dead terrorist was expected for further identification and fingerprinting by the C.I.D. He duly arrived. Apart from the gaping hole in his left side – the exit point of the single bullet that had ended his career as a terrorist – there was little to distinguish the dead man from any other young African. He was about 22-years-old and had spent almost as many days in his last employment – as an item of terrorist crash-course cannon fodder.

For the second time that day I was able to do something useful. It was dusk and the C.I.D. had no flash (since remedied). It's a long time since I had anything to do with dead bodies, particularly those with their intestines blown out – and secretly I wondered at my utter detachment as I peered through the view-finder for a close-up. Perhaps the few hours I had spent at the sharp end, or the aerial tour of Chaona Farm, had been sufficient acclimatisation. Still, I'm glad no one offered to let me fingerprint the dead terrorist.

That night I shared a room in a house situated in the village. The empty house had been taken over by the C.I.D. and the invitation to share the room contained more than a note of caution. I was told – at length – that the house was the last in the line of dwellings and that our particular bedroom was at the 'vulnerable' end of the house in the event we were attacked. It was scant consolation to receive a mild rocket for leaving my pistol locked up in the Charge Office, to watch the C.I.D. Land Rover being parked slap up against the window and to hear my room-mate cocking his F.N. as I clambered into my sleeping bag. Besides, the rifle could easily have been knocked over by a restless sleeper – but my companion slept much more soundly than did his room-mate.

Eight detectives queuing to use a single bathroom precipitates an early awakening. With the natural admiration of audience for actors, I waited until they had all finished before shaving. The hot water system in that house must be remarkably efficient but hot water is a luxury enjoyed by only a few policemen in the Centenary field of operations.

Breakfast at the *Queen Mary* – eggs, bacon and kidneys (the last provoking a fleeting recollection of the previous evening's photography) – was followed by plans for me to visit Mount Darwin. The flight with the Police Reserve Air Wing was a much more comfortable, and shorter, journey than if I had gone by road.

Mount Darwin is a much larger place than Centenary and there was a more obvious 'civilian' air about the place, despite the helicopter drooping in the District Commissioner's parking bay outside the Internal Affairs offices. Opposite the building are a few hectares of scrub with the police station beyond. It was from this unused land that the Internal Affairs complex had come under terrorist fire on the night of January 8. The superficial damage inflicted by the enemy had been quickly repaired.

On the morning's agenda was the weekly meeting between the security forces and the civilian authorities. Police represen-tation consisted of the Officer Commanding Mazoe Valley District, the Border Control Officer, members-in-charge of Mount Darwin and Bindura, Special Branch and C.I.D. officers and the Flight Commander Mazoe Valley Police Reserve Air Wing. With several army officers, the area airforce commander and three Internal Affairs representatives, there was little room to spare in the District Commissioner's conference room. I squeezed in and found the local interpretation of the overall security situation instructive and very interesting.

Obviously the discussions cannot be reported here.

The meeting took up most of the morning and midday brought with it the opportunity to sample the fare at Mount Darwin's 'Forces Canteen', a sort of impromptu N.A.A.F.I. which is loca-ted in and run by the ladies of Mount Darwin Club. Members of the forces can avail themselves of a number of five-cent dishes – a 'pinta' (milk), hotdog, hamburger, steak roll and so forth.

At this point it is worth mentioning the combined security force and civilian teams that are operating in the subverted areas of Northern Mashonaland and fulfilling a variety of functions. The teams consist of police officers, representatives of Internal Affairs and Lands Inspectorate and a protective army detachment. The most important police role with the complex is that of intelligence – questioning locals suspected of having assisted the terrorists, making arrests on the results of such interrogation, the initial documentation of detained persons and so forth.

One of these teams had returned to Mount Darwin that morning to off-load prisoners, re-provision, receive fresh instructions and to release a C.I.D. section officer who was wanted in Bulawayo by an impatient fiancée – he was getting married the following Saturday. I was to get a more intensive picture of the teams in operation the following day.

The permanent staff at Mount Darwin police station – as at Centenary – are in danger of being overlooked in the general excitement. The invaluable local knowledge of both European and African policemen permanently stationed in the area has resulted in many of them being spirited off to serve with the field teams. Those left behind have the rather sweeping role of keeping their stations running and this involves long radio watches – monitoring the almost ceaseless crackle on crowded frequencies – as well as keeping abreast of a host of quarter-master's responsibilities. Although ordinary crime hardly figures in the area, there are all sorts of investigations not specifically concerned with the emergency but indirectly caused by it and these duties fall on the shoulders of the reduced station complement. Again, it is not a glamorous role and in mid-February some of these policemen were taking their first time-off since Christmas.

My good deed for the day consisted in escorting a prisoner back to Centenary. He was an old man who looked deceptively harmless. The charge against him was that he had indicated to the terrorists fellow tribesmen who objected to the formers' subversive activities. His victims had been kidnapped, taken to terrorist bases in Mozambique and tortured.

I couldn't help wondering what my prisoner was thinking as he flew – almost certainly for the first time – in one of the most luxurious of the Air Wing's machines back to Centenary. His attitude to the flight was completely impassive.

The programme for my last day at the sharp end became definite when the police officer in charge of the field teams suggested that I accompany him to the Chiweshe Reserve, an area which had become increasingly important in the previous few days. A chilly helicopter flight took us to a school at the northern end of the T.T.L. where one of the field teams was based.

Chiweshe is a beautiful and prosperous-looking area. Fertile green valleys snuggle between the ever-present gomos. It looked peaceful enough but appearances can be – and in this case were – very deceptive. As the helicopter swooped between the grey granite hills surrounding the school, an armed squad of territorial servicemen doubled from the buildings to cover our landing. Defensive positions had been prepared and were still being dug in front of the two staggered lines of classrooms and administrative offices.

There were about a dozen European and African policemen at the school under the command of a Detective Inspector who had only recently been transferred to Salisbury C.I.D. from Special Branch, Bulawayo. It wasn't a particularly good time for introductions, he was trying to wrap up the initial interrogation of a captured local terrorist – the first live one I had seen so far. Like his dead companion and the old 'quisling' of the previous day, there was nothing remarkable about the prisoner. He was a sixteen-year-old youth whose demeanour, physique and clothing would have made him indistinguishable from the hundreds of scholars, garden boys or house servants seen on any weekend in Salisbury. He was neither arrogant or contrite. He just seemed a little mesmerised at the seriousness with which his activities over the past few weeks were being viewed by the police. He would have driven the most experienced television interviewer mad with frustration. Eventually he was passed up the line to field headquarters for more questioning.

With the immediate pressures off, there was time to observe more closely the police role in this situation. I sat in on one of the interrogation sessions for a while – until the interviewer asked me to leave. Apparently the presence of a silent spectator was not helping his concentration. In print I formally apologise. In retrospect, day after day of this type of investigation plainly is not helped by an audience and I had innocently put my foot in, and my finger on, perhaps the most important and basic fact of police work at the sharp end. It involves nothing more than hour upon hour of endless questions and answers, a frustrating business at the best of times but in the current type of operation, even more exasperating.

Purely as an illustration of how time-consuming and unrewarding these duties are, let me quote the case of the five young African women who were detained on suspicion of having fed and warmed the beds of a particular terrorist gang. At first they had denied the charges. Later, in circumstances which had made their separate confinement totally impossible, they had concocted a story of the hospitality they had given to a group of seven terrorists. The women had rehearsed their stories, complete with identities, to the point of perfection while the C.I.D. team were engaged in questioning more important witnesses. Their fairy tale was made even more plausible by coincidence. The names they recited as recipients of their favours included two of the known nicknames of the gang under investigation, as well as the real name of the captured local who was related to one of the women. Only after a day's persistent questioning by different members of the police team was the terrorist's story confirmed – that he had never seen the women before apart from the one to whom he was related. The women's list of names was little more than an African equivalent of the Tom, Dick and Harry variety. The reason the women thought up the story is even harder to understand. They thought they would be released if they told the police they had been consorting with the gang.

The incident is a pointer to the future requirements from the police point of view if, as seems likely, this type of terrorist activity becomes protracted. Only policemen have the professional background and experience to answer this increasing need for patient, intelligent investigators, men who are prepared to ask question after question dispassionately for hours on end if necessary, men who are thereafter capable of assessing the truth and value of their investigations. In the past, massive police drives have been successful in reaping a bumper crop of suspects. There is certainly no shortage of suspects at the moment, nor is there a critical lack of harvesters. But when it comes down to sorting the wheat from the chaff, the ordinary experienced policeman comes into his own. He doesn't have to be an expert shot, or a superbly fit athlete capable of covering kilometres per hour in the bush. He must be no more and no less than a dependable, patient and intelligent investigator. And there is precious little glamour in the role. One thing that was most noticeable while watching the field team at work was the tremendous co-operation given to the police by this particular army territorial unit. Not only did they do nearly all the leg-work while the policemen got on with the interrogations, but they did so with a great deal of initiative. Locating a string of suspects is never an easy matter in the rural areas but these soldiers followed up one lead after another, without specific police direction, usually to a satisfactory outcome.

Together with an Internal Affairs officer who had also spent the day in Chiweshe consulting with his subordinates, I was choppered out of the T.T.L. in mid-afternoon. The day was almost over for those left behind. Supper is consumed before dark and the night is a long watchful one. The sun sets behind a solitary pillar of rock which is said to be an object of reverence for the local tribesmen. It is looked upon with suspicion by those members of the security forces familiar with the enemy's propensity for witchcraft.

The flight back to Centenary was prolonged in order to execute a leaflet-dropping mission over Chiweshe's northern kraals. In the rear centre seat of the helicopter, I couldn't help with the drop and so lost the chance of a hat-trick of constructive tasks during my three days at the sharp end.

Centenary looked very peaceful as we landed and it was fairly obvious that there had been no excitement during the day. It had been business as usual with the C.I.D. and Special Branch teams questioning innumerable suspects, with Centenary Control finding a few more dozen obscure places on the huge wall map. A new *Queen Mary* crew had certainly prepared the correct quota of meals and innumerable urns of tea and coffee. A few more hours had been logged by the police air wing pilots and their observers, the majority of those hours being spent in the tiring role of providing link communications between various ground patrols. The erotic literature jealously guarded by the Rhodesian Air Force control had, despite their efforts, become more thumbed-through and exclaimed at.

The station's own 'Q' branch representative had been relieved and replaced and the incumbent had no doubt spent the day trying to equate the number of beers remaining with the kitty, or manipulating the extremely efficient 'T&S' system which meant that policemen leaving for a rest-cure in the bright lights could do so with something in their pockets. Among these was a C.I.D. section officer who had been stationed at the foot of the Zambesi Escarpment for several weeks, down there at the tip of the sharp end, but he was long gone in the pursuits of the delights of civilisation which he had anticipated so descriptively over the previous evening's beer.

As I walked from the airfield past the police mess, the C.M.E.D. mechanic was groping with the innards of yet another Land Rover, one of the few individuals among some many different teams. The road between the airfield and the police station was being graded – even the rural council was getting in on the act – and to the left was the air force conglomeration of tents and caravans, on the right the massive sprawling might of the army. Scattered between were the bits and pieces of Internal Affairs, Lands Inspectorate, Parks and Wild Life Department. Individually they had marched and driven and questioned, together they had consulted to add a few more pieces to the complicated jigsaw puzzle of Northern Mashonaland.

I gathered my gear, proffered my thanks for what was, in the circumstances, very generous hospitality, and made a last vain search for Centenary's mascot, 'Wee Jock Thunderstorm', the diminutive little puppy that was the property of one of the air force pilots, the friend of everyone for miles, and the scourge of the other dogs in camp – but curiously camera-shy.

As I drove south to Concession, I wondered what I could say about the last three days, what I would be allowed to write. If some sort of personal reaction is admissible, things are not as gloomy as the rumour-mongers would have us believe, which is not to deny the existence of a war of sobering reality. Those at the sharp end have had to come to terms with some very nasty facts of life. Continually faced with these problems through long hard days and short nights, with prospects for an early return to normality remote, the policemen at the sharp end can be forgiven for the strained look they wear. Perhaps tomorrow they will be smiling.

Air Force Alouette and crew take a break in typical operating terrain